The Trench Cat of Ypres

1917

Jack Champion

Copyright © 2025 by Jack Champion

All rights reserved.

No part of this book may be reproduced, stored in a retrieval system, or transmitted in any form or by any means—electronic, mechanical, photocopying, recording, or otherwise —without the prior written permission of the publisher, except for brief quotations in critical reviews or articles.

ISBN 978-1-918219-54-8

First Edition: 2025
Published by: Cosmic Jive Publishing

www.cosmicjivepublishing.com

For permissions and inquiries, contact:
info@cosmicjivepublishing.com

Disclaimer:

This is a work of fiction inspired by historical events of the First World War. While the setting reflects real conditions of the era, all characters—including the cat—are fictional. Names, places, events, and incidents are either products of the author's imagination or are used fictitiously. Any resemblance to actual persons, living or dead, or to real events is purely coincidental.

Ypres Salient, 1917

Chapter 1
A Pennyworth of Luck

PRIVATE THOMAS "TOMMY" FINCH paid a whole shilling for the cat. It was a fortune to a lad from the Durham coalfields—a week's pay gone in a moment's stubborn decision. Back home, a shilling could buy three pints of bitter, a week's rent for a collier's cottage, or a decent pair of secondhand boots. Here, in the Ypres Salient in the autumn of 1917, it bought nothing but mud, fear, and the occasional bottle of sour plonk from the estaminets.

But the French farmer's boy had been insistent, holding the scruffy creature out like a prize goose, his eyes wide with a blend of desperation and cunning.

"Bon chat, monsieur! Très bon pour les rats!" The boy's trousers were three inches too short, and his knees were the colour of the surrounding clay. Behind him, what remained of his family's farmhouse showed a jagged silhouette against the Flanders sky—one wall standing, the rest a tumble of bricks and memory.

Tommy's mates were watching, their breath making ghosts in the chill air.

"A shillin' for a bag o' bones an' fleas, Finch? Yer daft as a brush," snorted Alfie, his best mate, as Tommy handed over the coin.

The money changed hands—a bright, new King's shilling for this muddy, miserable corner of Belgium.

The boy scampered off as if expecting the transaction to be reversed, and Tommy was left holding a surprisingly heavy, spitting ball of ginger fur.

"He's not for cuddlin'," Tommy said, more to himself than to Alfie, as the cat writhed in his grasp, all claws and outrage. "He's for the rats."

That was the official line, the sensible reason. The trenches around the Ypres Salient were a rat empire. They grew fat on the unending grim harvest—bold as brass, some as big as terriers, with sleek grey coats and eyes that gleamed in the dark. They gnawed on the dead and stole from the living with equal impartiality. Just last week, Tommy had woken to find one nibbling at the dried beef in his haversack, right beside his head. Another had made off with Private Perkins' last pair of dry socks, dragging them through the mud like a prize banner.

The rats rustled through the dugouts, their squeaks and scuttles a constant, maddening chorus beneath the thunder of the guns. They danced across sleeping men's chests, bred in the latrines, and watched with bright, intelligent eyes as soldiers wrote letters home.

A good ratter was worth its weight in bully beef, and even the officers turned a blind eye to the unofficial mascots if they kept the vermin down.

But as Tommy tucked the struggling cat inside his greatcoat—a maneuver that earned him three fresh scratches on his wrist—and felt the vibration of its low, warning growl against his chest, he knew the truth was simpler, and softer. He was lonely.

He was nineteen, but felt ninety. The mud had seeped into his soul, a thick, cloying presence that coated everything from his boots to his dreams. The noise had deadened his ears—not just the big guns, but the constant background chorus: the drip of water, the cough of the man next to you, the rustle of rats, the distant ping of a sniper's bullet off the parapet. And the sight of his twin brother, taken by a sniper at Passchendaele Ridge just three months prior, haunted his every blink. Not the heroic death of the recruiting posters—no flag in hand, no noble last words—just a sudden red spray against the mud, and then silence where Billy's laughter used to be.

Tommy needed something to be responsible for that wasn't just staying alive. Something that was alive, and solely his. Not a piece of machinery to be cleaned, not a section of trench to be maintained, not even a comrade to watch over (though he did that too, instinctively). Something small. Something that didn't understand the war.

He carried the cat back to the dugout, a low, earthy cave that housed ten men and smelled perpetually of damp wool, tobacco, and the faint, sweet-sickly undertone of decay. The dugout was their castle—eight feet by ten, with bunks stacked like shelves in a larder, a makeshift table of ammunition boxes, and a brazier that glowed with a precious, grudging heat.

"Christ, Finch, what've you brought in now?" asked Sergeant Mackay, looking up from cleaning his Webley revolver. The sergeant had a face like old leather, creased and weathered, with eyes that missed nothing.

"Ratter, Sarge," Tommy said, trying to sound matter-of-fact.

Mackay grunted. "Better be. I'm not having another of Perkins' bloody mice." Private Perkins, the youngest of their section at seventeen, had tried to tame a field mouse two weeks prior. It had promptly disappeared into the wall, followed by a family of its relatives who seemed to find the dugout quite hospitable.

Tommy found an empty ammunition crate and lined it with a scrap of blanket from his pack. He set the cat inside. It immediately flattened itself against the back, a low growl rumbling in its throat. In the dim candlelight, he could see it properly for the first time: not a tom, but a queen, he realized now. A scrawny thing, all ribs and spine beneath the muddy ginger fur, with one ear notched from some old fight. Her eyes were the colour of bottle glass, wide with fear and fury.

"Looks half-starved," said Alfie, peering over Tommy's shoulder. "Probably got worms, too. And fleas. Definitely got fleas."

"She'll fatten up," Tommy said, more hope than conviction.

He named her Penny. Partly for the shilling, partly because he hoped she'd bring a pennyworth of luck—a small, modest fortune in a place where fortune was measured in surviving the next hour, the next day, the next patrol.

Penny wanted nothing to do with him, the trench, or the war. For three days, she resided in a cranny behind Tommy's bunk, a space so small he hadn't known it existed until she found it. Only the gleam of her eyes in the candlelight betrayed her presence. Her meals—pilfered sardines (a luxury Tommy traded his rum ration for), hardtack crumbs soaked in condensed milk, and once, a precious bit of bacon rind—were taken with a sullen snatch. She offered no purr, no rub, no acknowledgment beyond a baleful stare.

"Told you," Alfie said on the third evening, puffing on a Woodbine that filled the dugout with its acrid smoke. "Ungrateful mog. Should've bought a ferret. At least a ferret'd be useful. And you can train 'em."

"To do what?" asked Perkins, looking up from the letter he was writing home. "Fetch sticks?"

"To bite Germans, you daft apt," Alfie retorted. "Tie a message to its neck, send it across no-man's land. 'Dear

Fritz, we're coming over Thursday, love, Tommy.'"

A ripple of tired laughter went through the dugout. It was the kind of joke that wasn't funny, but they laughed anyway because the alternative was screaming.

Then the rats came.

It was after stand-to, when the men were eating their evening stew—a watery, grey concoction of bully beef, desiccated vegetables, and the omnipresent mud. A big, sleek brute of a rat, grey as a battleship and just as confident, waddled across the floor of the dugout. It moved with a proprietor's air, heading straight for Tommy's haversack where he'd stored a precious tin of apricot jam sent from home.

Before Tommy could even move his foot, a ginger streak shot from the shadows. There was no heroic battle, no dramatic tussle. It was a brief, brutal, and efficient silence. A pounce that seemed to defy physics—a blur of movement ending in a sharp, decisive snap. The rat went limp. Penny, with a disdainful flick of her tail, dragged her prize back into her cranny to dine in private, as if embarrassed by her own vulgar display of utility.

The men in the dugout stared, their spoons frozen halfway to their mouths. Then they erupted—not into cheers, exactly, but into something rougher, more relieved.

"Blimey! She's a proper little sergeant-major, she is!" Alfie clapped Tommy on the back so hard he nearly choked on his stew. "Did you see that? Faster than a whippet!"

"Quiet, you lot," growled Sergeant Mackay, but even he was smiling, a rare crack in the granite. "Let the creature eat in peace. Might get us another."

From that night on, Penny's status changed. She was no longer Tommy's failed investment; she was the dugout's resident exterminator, a tiny, furry piece of essential trench kit.

The men started leaving offerings by her cranny—a bit of cheese from a parcel, the fatty end of a sausage, a spoonful of milk saved from the morning tea. She accepted these tributes with the same regal indifference, but her presence became a fixture.

She never became affectionate, not in the way the tales spoke of dogs like Corporal, the Airedale terrier who'd become a regimental mascot and been written up in *The Times*. She didn't follow Tommy on patrol or lick his wounds. Her loyalty, he came to understand, was to the territory—their small, foul-smelling stretch of trench and dugout. She tolerated Tommy because he was the primary bringer of sardines and occupied the warmest spot by the brazier. But her companionship was a silent, sideways thing.

She would sit on the firestep beside him during the quiet hours before dawn, a still, watchful presence while he smoked a cigarette, the glow of it the only light in the world. Her ears twitched at sounds too distant for human ears—the scuttle of a rat three traverses down, the creak of a periscope being raised, the almost-inaudible whisper of the wind changing direction.

Sometimes, in the dead of night when the shelling was distant and the trench was quiet except for the snores of exhausted men, she would curl in the hollow of his legs as he tried to sleep. She was a small furnace of warmth against the damp chill that seeped through the groundsheet and blankets. It was, he felt, a kind of truce—an agreement between two creatures that they would share this space, this moment of relative safety, without demanding more of each other than they could give.

Her real talent, however, was observation. The rats

The Trench Cat of Ypres

were her business, but she noticed everything. Tommy learned to read her like the officers read their maps. When Penny's ears flattened against her skull and she vanished into her cranny, a shelling was coming, sometimes minutes before the first distant *crump* reached them. When she sat bolt upright on the firestep, staring intently at a section of parapet, it often meant movement in no-man's land—a British patrol returning, or worse, a German raiding party forming up in their own trenches. She was their early-warning system, more reliable than any sentry made weary by boredom and fear.

One frozen morning in late November, when the duckboards were slick with ice and the breath hung in clouds before men's faces, a new lieutenant arrived. He came with the rations party, a fresh-faced boy named Chambers, straight from Sandhurst, with a zeal for regulations that was painful to behold. He couldn't have been more than twenty, but he carried himself with the stiffness of a man twice his age, as if his spine had been replaced with a ruler.

Lieutenant Chambers decided the dugout was "a disgrace" and ordered a thorough clean-out. "This isn't a pigsty, Sergeant!" he declared, his voice too loud in the confined space. "I want these floors scraped, these walls tidied, and all personal effects stowed properly!"

In the chaos that followed—men shuffling their meagre possessions, sweeping out months of accumulated dirt and discarded tins—Penny was chased out by a well-meaning but clodhopping private with a broom. The private, a new replacement from London named Davies, had been told to "clear out any vermin" and had taken this to include the cat.

Tommy didn't see her go. He was on latrine duty—the worst of all fatigues—digging a new slit trench while trying not to breathe through his nose. By the time he returned, his hands numb and his uniform stinking, the dugout smelled overpoweringly of carbolic and damp stone. And Penny was gone.

"Where is she?" he asked, trying to keep the panic from his voice.

"Davies chased her out with a broom," Alfie said, not looking up from cleaning his rifle. "She'll be back for her supper."

But Alfie's voice lacked conviction. Tommy's heart, an organ he thought long numbed by the daily business of survival, dropped like a stone into the mud of his boots. He'd lost his twin brother to this war. He'd watched friends vanish into the mud of Passchendaele. Now he'd lost his cat to a broom and a boy lieutenant's zeal for cleanliness.

Night fell, a thick, icy blackness that seemed to swallow sound as well as light. The wind whistled down the trench, finding every gap in clothing, every chink in the spirit. The usual rat-scuffles were absent, as if the vermin themselves were holding their breath. The dugout felt emptier than ever—not just of the cat, but of something vital, a small, warm presence that had made the place feel less like a grave.

Tommy sat on his bunk, a piece of salted pork in his hand (saved from his rations for her), feeling a foolish, gaping loss. It was disproportionate, he knew. Men were dying by the thousands. A cat was nothing. And yet.

Just before dawn, as he took his turn on watch, peering into the shifting gloom of no-man's land through a periscope, he heard it. Not a meow, but a familiar, chittering sound Penny made when she had a particularly large rat cornered—a rapid, excited clicking of her teeth. It came from just beyond the parapet, in the twisted waste between the lines.

Tommy froze, his breath catching. He peered into the gloom, his eyes straining. There, in a shattered shell-hole about thirty yards out, a flicker of movement. Ginger fur, pale in the nascent light. Penny was out there, stalking something in the deadly ground between the lines.

And as Tommy watched, horrified, he saw something else. A faint, metallic glint in a different shell-hole, twenty yards to the left. A German helmet, catching the first weak light. A listening post, or a sniper, settled in for the dawn watch.

Penny, intent on her hunt, was creeping directly into the line of sight.

Tommy's mouth went dry, the taste of last night's stew turning sour. The cat wasn't a hero. She was just a cat. A hungry, pragmatic creature now leading a German's eye right towards a vulnerable stretch of their own trench. There was no grand rescue possible, no daring dash over the top. To call out was to give away his own position and invite a bullet from the very sniper he was trying to avoid.

All he could do was watch, and whisper a desperate, silent plea into the frozen air.

"Penny," he breathed, the steam of his words snatched by the wind. "For God's sake... just be a cat. Be lucky."

He readied his rifle, not to fire (the sound would bring down hell), but because holding it gave him something to do with his hands. His eyes darted between the two specks in the devastation—one a tiny, ignorant life, the other a hidden death. The first pale light of day began to bleed into the sky, turning the world a sickly grey. The war, for a moment, had shrunk to this: a man, his cat, and the terrible, waiting silence.

Chapter 2
The Listeners

THE GINGER STREAK in no-man's land froze. Penny had pinned her quarry—a large, twitching field rat grown fat on the unburied dead—against a fragment of splintered timber that had once been part of a Belgian barn. Her world had shrunk to the kill: the heat of the creature beneath her paws, the rapid thrum of its terrified heart, the musky scent of its fear.

Tommy's world had expanded to include the glint of the German helmet, the faintest suggestion of a human shape in the shadows of the shell crater. He held his breath, the cold metal of his Lee-Enfield's stock biting into his cheek. Every instinct screamed to duck, to shout, to fire a warning shot into the air. But movement was death. Sound was death. In this place, even a cough could earn you a sniper's bullet through the forehead.

He was a statue of mud and dread, praying to a God he wasn't sure listened in this godforsaken corner of Flanders. He prayed not for a miracle, but for something smaller: that a cat would remember it was time for breakfast.

The seconds drew out, heavy and unyielding. Somewhere down the line, a machine gun tapped out a brief, conversational burst—*tat-tat-tat*—then fell silent. The wind shifted, carrying the smell of cordite and the deeper, more disturbing scent of the Salient itself: wet earth, rotting wood, and something sweetly chemical that might have been gas lingering in a low-lying crater.

In the German shell-hole, something shifted. A periscope—just a subtle rustle of cloth against the crater's lip, the faintest gleam of glass. The German was watching, but his focus, Tommy realized with a surge of something that wasn't quite hope, wasn't on the British parapet. He was watching the cat.

Tommy saw the man's head turn slightly, a pale oval under the helmet's rim, following Penny's cautious, stalking movements. For a bizarre, suspended moment, the war consisted of two hidden men and one utterly indifferent animal—a surreal tableau in the grey dawn.

Penny pounced. There was a faint, final squeak, lost in the vast silence of the morning. She stood over her prize, a small, triumphant silhouette against the crater's lip, her tail held high like a banner. Then, with the practicality of her kind, she picked up the rat in her jaws—it was nearly as big as her head—and turned. Not back towards the British line, but parallel to it, seeking a quiet, sheltered spot to eat her hard-won breakfast.

She walked directly past the German's shell-hole, so close the man could have reached out and touched her with his bayonet.

Tommy's finger tightened on the trigger, the pad of his index finger going white with pressure. He saw the German's helmet dip as he tracked her progress. And then he heard it—a low, muffled chuckle. A human sound, startling in the lunar silence of no-man's land. The German was *amused.*

The tension in Tommy's shoulders unlocked by a fraction, though his rifle remained aimed. A man who laughed at a cat hunting a rat was, for this second, not a man sighting down a barrel at him. He was just a man, watching a cat. A man just like him.

And in that ordinary, unguarded sound, Tommy saw the rest of him—boots caked with the same mud, hands as raw and work-worn as his own. A man who had once risen before dawn to labour, who knew the weight of tools and the ache that settled in the bones at day's end. A man who might have sisters, or a mother who kept a small kitchen clean against the odds, or a cat that slept by the fire and hunted mice in a shed. A man who may have lost his brother to this madness.

A man who would remember this moment later, if he lived, not as mercy or pity, but simply as something human that had survived the war for the space of a breath.

Penny disappeared into a tangle of rusted wire that sprouted from the mud like metallic brambles. The German's periscope withdrew with a last, almost reluctant movement. The moment broke, dissipating like mist. The grey dawn light solidified, revealing the full, terrible landscape in all its hideous detail: the overlapping craters like suppurating sores on the earth's skin, the black ribs of shattered trees, the pale, waxen forms that weren't mud at all if you looked too closely.

The listening post was now known, marked on Tommy's mental map with a cold, clear X. He slithered down from the firestep, his muscles protesting after the long stillness, his heart hammering against his ribs like it wanted out.

"Anything?" Alfie asked, materialising from the gloom of the trench like a spectre. He handed Tommy a tin mug of over-stewed tea, the liquid the colour of mud and almost as thick.

"Just a cat," Tommy said, his voice rough from disuse and the cold. "And a Jerry who fancied a laugh."

Alfie raised an eyebrow, the gesture exaggerated in the

The Trench Cat of Ypres

poor light. His face was a collection of shadows and stubble, his eyes red-rimmed from lack of sleep. "A laugh? Bloody hell. What's he got to laugh about? His turn in this shithole come up?"

"Penny caught a rat. A big 'un. Walked right past his hole."

Alfie stared at him, then let out a soft whistle. "Cheeky bugger. She's got more nerve than that Lieutenant Chambers." He took a sip from his own mug, grimaced, and spat onto the duckboards. "Christ, this tea's got more grit in it than a colliery floor."

Someone was singing softly, off-key—a music hall tune Tommy remembered his mother humming, back when her eyes still smiled, in the life that existed before he and his twin went off to the war. *"...down at the old Bull and Bush..."* Further down, two men were arguing in low, fierce whispers about a missing pair of socks. The trench had its own rules, its own economy, its own fragile ecosystem. Some truths, like a German soldier laughing at a cat, were too delicate, too human, to speak aloud. They belonged to the strange, quiet moments between the shelling.

Penny returned two hours later, sauntering down the trench as if she'd been for a stroll up on the Durham moors out towards Weardale rather than hunting in a landscape of death. She had a new notch of confidence in her stride, a certain swagger in the twitch of her tail. The men of the section, emerging for their own meagre breakfasts, greeted her like a returning raider.

"There she is! The great hunter of Plugstreet!" called out Perkins, his face still soft with youth despite the grime.

"Got us a four-pounder for the pot, did ya, Pen?" joked another man, Johnson, a former butcher from Leeds who missed his trade almost as much as he missed his family.

She ignored them all, her regal indifference intact. She headed straight for Tommy, who was sitting on an upturned crate trying to coax a flame from a damp match for his cigarette. At his boots, she dropped the thoroughly deceased and somewhat mangled rat. It wasn't a gift. It was, he understood with sudden clarity, a tax payment. Rent for the sardines, for the warm spot by the brazier, for her place in the dugout.

"Cheers," Tommy muttered, using the toe of his boot to discreetly nudge the offering into a nearby sump hole where it sank with a soft *plop*. Penny gave a raspy *mrrp* of what might have been approval, or perhaps just acknowledgment of a transaction completed, and began meticulously washing a muddy paw, starting between the toes with fastidious care.

From that day, her role in the section solidified. She was their unorthodox sentry, their furry barometer of the front. Her hunts took her regularly to the edges of no-man's land—never far, but far enough to see and hear things the men in the trench could not. Her behaviour upon return became a kind of crude, vital intelligence.

A relaxed wash in a patch of weak sunlight meant all quiet. Ears perpetually twitching, fur slightly puffed along the spine—there was movement out there, men shifting in trenches, working parties, something. A sudden, skittish retreat into the deepest recesses of the dugout, hiding under Tommy's bunk, meant incoming shells, her sensitive ears catching the distant scream of the projectiles seconds, sometimes a full minute, before the men could.

Lieutenant Chambers, the new officer, remained unimpressed. "Unhygienic," he sniffed one afternoon, watching Penny shred a rat near the latrine with single-minded intensity. "We're soldiers, not zookeepers. This isn't the bloody London Zoological Gardens."

The men within earshot stiffened, but said nothing. It was Sergeant Mackay who spoke, his voice a low, gravelly rumble that carried authority without needing volume.

"With respect, sir," he said, not looking up from the map he was studying, "that creature's worth two sentries. She hears things we don't. Picks up the vibrations, like. And the rats..." He finally glanced at the Lieutenant. "Well, you've seen the rations are poor enough without them getting a share. Had a tin of Machonochie last week, opened it up, found a rat had got there first. Nasty business."

Chambers had indeed seen the size of the trench rats. He'd also, despite himself, seen the way the men's spirits lifted when the cat was around. Morale was a vague concept in the training manuals, something about *esprit de corps* and regimental pride. But here it was, made flesh and fur—a small, ginger creature whose presence made the men smile, made them save scraps despite their own hunger, gave them something to talk about other than death and mud. It was a tiny rebellion against the dehumanising grind.

He gave a stiff, almost imperceptible nod. "Just keep *it* out of my dugout." He said it as if the officer's dugout—a slightly larger, marginally drier hole in the ground—was the Royal Suite at the Ritz.

Penny, of course, took this as a personal invitation. That very evening, after Chambers had retired to write his nightly letter home (his pen scratching furiously, as if he could write his way out of this place), she was found curled on the Lieutenant's spare greatcoat, which was draped over a crate. She had made a perfect circle of warmth and shed ginger hair on the dark wool.

Private Davies, the broom-wielder, saw her first and froze, eyes wide. "Sir, the cat—"

Chambers looked up from his writing, his face tight with irritation. Then he saw her. For a long moment, he just stared. Then, the Lieutenant simply sighed—a long, weary, bone-deep sound that made him seem suddenly much older than his twenty years. It was the sigh of a man who has realized that some battles are not worth fighting, that some rules break against the simple, stubborn reality of life persisting.

He didn't throw her out. He just sat back down, dipped his pen in the ink, and continued his letter. Penny opened one eye, deemed him harmless, and went back to sleep, her purr a soft rumble in the quiet space.

The incident became trench legend, told and retold. "You hear about the cat and the Lieutenant?" ... "She's got him trained proper, she has." It was a small victory, a tiny crack in the rigid hierarchy, and it made the men love her all the more.

The winter hardened its grip. The incessant rain turned to sleet, then to a fine, needling snow that did nothing to hide the mud, only made it colder. The ground froze into a jagged, iron-hard landscape of ruts and craters, each footprint a potential twisted ankle. Penny grew a thicker coat, a luxurious ruff of fur around her neck, and spent more time pressed against the meagre heat sources: the brazier, a man's back, the steam from a mess tin.

Her forays into no-man's land became less frequent, her world contracting to the dugout, the firestep, and the winding communication trench that led to the cookhouse —a journey she sometimes made with Tommy, trotting at his heels like a tiny, furry shadow, much to the amusement of the cooks.

The Trench Cat of Ypres

It was during one of these routine ration parties through that communication trench that it happened. The trench was narrow there, the walls oozing a constant trickle of icy water. Tommy, Alfie, Perkins, and two others were making their way back, laden with sandbags full of tins, loaves of stale bread, and a precious can of paraffin for the brazier. The sky was a uniform grey, the air still and heavy.

The shell came without the usual warning scream—a sudden, shrieking "whizz-bang" from a German 77mm field gun. It was designed to arrive before the sound of its firing, and it did so with murderous efficiency. It landed with a deafening, concussive *CRACK* twenty yards behind them, in the trench they'd just vacated.

The world dissolved. Noise became a solid thing, punching the air from Tommy's lungs. Flying earth, splinters of wood, and chunks of frozen mud rained down. He was thrown forward into the slimy wall of the trench, his face pressed into the cold clay, the breath knocked from him in a painful grunt. For a moment, there was only ringing silence and the taste of dirt.

Then the sounds rushed back in: Alfie swearing in a continuous, creative stream; the groans of a man hit— Private Johnson, clutching his leg where a piece of shrapnel had torn through his puttee; and the cooks further back shouting in alarm.

And another sound. A high, furious, hair-raising yowl of pure terror.

Tommy's head snapped around, mud falling from his hair. Penny, who had been shadowing them for scraps, was a bristling, spitting arc of fury and fear. A chunk of shrapnel the size of a man's fist had torn through the sandbag she'd been sitting beside, missing her by inches. It had also, in its passing, severed the leather strap of

Tommy's haversack, which now lay open and gaping like a wounded mouth. Its contents—his spare socks, his paybook, a photograph of his mother, and his last, precious tin of sardines, hoarded for a special occasion that never came—spilled out into the foul, icy water swirling at the bottom of the trench.

For a second, man and cat stared at the same sight: the small, blue tin sinking into the murk, bubbles rising from it. The sardines were gone.

Then Penny, driven by a storm of fear and indignant, profound loss, did not run back towards the relative safety of the dugout. She bolted forward, down the communication trench, away from the blast site, towards the front line and the increasing thunder of the guns.

"Penny! No!" Tommy's shout was lost in the whistle of another incoming shell, this one further down the line. He scrambled to his feet, ignoring the stinging cut on his brow where he'd hit the wall.

Johnson was being tended to. The ration party was in disarray. His duty, as a soldier, was here. But his cat—his stupid, ungrateful, essential cat—was running *towards* *t*he guns, towards the place where the world was most actively trying to end itself.

He saw the flick of her ginger tail disappear around a traverse. He made a choice, the kind that makes no sense anywhere but in the twisted logic of the trench.

Grabbing his rifle from where it had fallen, he shouted to Alfie, "Tell Sarge I'm checking the forward listening post!" It was a flimsy excuse, transparent as glass, but it was all he had.

Then he took off, his boots slipping on the duckboards, after a vanishing scrap of ginger fur. He was running, headlong, into the heart of the gathering storm, for a creature that had never once sat on his lap, that showed

The Trench Cat of Ypres

affection only through the absence of hostility. It was madness.

In the world of the trench, it was the only sanity left.

Chapter 3
The Sap

THE COMMUNICATION TRENCH was a river of churned mud and panic. Men clattered past Tommy, going the other way—their faces grey masks of urgency beneath their helmets. Some hauled boxes of ammunition, the weight bending their backs. Others stumbled under the weight of a stretcher bearing a groaning man whose uniform was dark with blood that wasn't mud. The air, already foul, now tasted of cordite and wet earth and the sharp, metallic tang of fresh fear.

Another shell screamed over, a different note—deeper, more freight-train roar than the whizz-bang's shriek. It landed somewhere in the support lines behind them with a sickening *crump* that vibrated through the duckboards under Tommy's feet. He ducked instinctively, shoulders hunched to his ears, a posture learned in his first week at the front and never unlearned. Dirt and pebbles rattled down from the parapet.

He'd lost sight of Penny almost immediately. She was a dart of shadow against shadow, a low, ginger streak moving with a speed born of primal terror. The explosion, the loss of her sardines, the sheer violent disruption of her world—it had overridden all the careful, wary habits she'd learned in months of trench life. She wasn't running to anywhere, only *away*—away from the blast, the noise, the incomprehensible water that had swallowed her prize.

"Stupid mog," he muttered, the words lost in the din as he pushed past a signaller hunched over a spool of wire, frantically trying to reconnect a line. The man didn't look up, his world shrunk to the two frayed ends in his filthy fingers.

Tommy's breath came in ragged gasps, pluming in the cold air. The front line here was a maze, a chaotic labyrinth dug by desperation and held by exhaustion. There were fire trenches, support trenches, communication trenches, saps—thin, precarious fingers poked out towards the enemy lines for listening posts or mining operations. It was a warren, a deadly honeycomb. She could be anywhere in it. Or worse, she could be *nowhere*—a red smear on a wall, a small body in a flooded crater.

He passed the turn for their own dugout. He could hear Sergeant Mackay's roar above the sporadic gunfire, a sound like bedrock splitting. "Johnson! Get that Lewis gun to traverse C! Davies, you useless article, sandbags on that breach! Move!" His duty was there, in the organized defense. His feet, acting on a logic deeper than duty, kept moving forward, deeper into the storm.

Ahead, the main trench narrowed, then forked. One branch continued along the front line, bustling with activity. The other became a forward sap—a dead-end tunnel barely shoulder-width, unrevetted here, its walls raw, weeping clay. It was a place of profound vulnerability, rarely manned in daylight except by listeners on the graveyard shift. A death-trap. It was also, Tommy realized with a cold certainty, exactly the kind of dark, confined, quiet place a terrified animal would bolt for.

He hesitated at the sap's entrance. It was like staring down a throat. The contrast was jarring: behind him, the chaotic symphony of the trench; ahead, a dripping, claustrophobic silence. The sap was a forgotten vein in the body of the war.

"Penny?" he hissed, his voice swallowed by the damp clay walls. No answering meow. Just the constant, maddening *drip-drip-drip* of water from the roof and the distant, rolling thunder of the barrage, which now seemed to be shifting, walking its fire deeper behind their lines, searching for batteries and supply dumps.

Cursing under his breath—a litany of profanity learned in the Durham pits and perfected in Flanders—he edged in. He held his rifle awkwardly before him, but it felt ridiculous in the narrow space, more a hindrance than a weapon. The sap was only just wider than his shoulders, the floor a shallow stream of icy water that soaked through his puttees immediately. The ceiling was so low he had to crouch.

After ten yards, the world behind him vanished around a slight bend. The sounds of the main trench became muffled, distant, like hearing a riot through a thick blanket. Here, the silence was a living thing, thick and pressing. It was the silence of a tomb, broken only by the drip of water and the frantic drum of his own heart in his ears.

He saw the scratch marks first. Fresh, frantic gouges in the clay wall at a point where a timber prop had partially collapsed, creating a small hollow, a natural alcove just big enough for a man to squeeze into. And there, curled into a tight, trembling ball in that hollow, was Penny.

Her fur was matted with mud and something darker. Her eyes, when she opened them at his approach, were wide, black pools of pure, undiluted fear. She wasn't spitting or growling. She was utterly frozen, paralyzed not just by the immediate terror, but by the enormity of the violence she'd fled—a violence that had followed her even here, to this quiet, dark place. She looked, for the first time since he'd known her, small. Not just in size, but in spirit.

"Alright, you daft thing," Tommy whispered, his anger at her flight evaporating into a wave of sheer, staggering relief that left him weak-kneed. "Got yourself in a proper pickle, haven't you?"

He slung his rifle over his shoulder with a soft clatter that made her flinch. Moving slowly, telegraphing his every motion, he reached for her. She didn't react, didn't hiss, just watched him with those huge, terrified eyes. He managed to get his hands around her, feeling the rapid-fire, hummingbird beat of her heart against his palms. It was a frantic, fragile rhythm. He tucked her inside his greatcoat, against the rough wool of his tunic, trying to envelop her in warmth and the familiar scent of tobacco, sweat, and home. She didn't struggle. Just buried her face into the fabric, a faint, continuous shiver running through her small frame like a minor earthquake.

He had to get back. Now. The sap was a cul-de-sac. With Penny a hard, trembling lump against his chest, he turned, the water sloshing around his boots.

As he did, the world outside the sap exploded.

Not with shells this time, but with a new, closer cacophony that turned his blood to ice. Sharp, guttural shouts in German. The distinctive *crack-crack-crack* of Mauser rifles, faster and higher-pitched than their Lee-Enfields. The hollow *pop* of stick grenades—'potato mashers'—followed by their deeper, dirtier explosions.

A raiding party. They'd used the cover of the German barrage to sneak across no-man's land. Now they were in the trench, hitting a weak point, seeking prisoners, creating chaos.

Running was impossible. The sap was a dead end. If he went out, he'd run straight into them. His mind, cold and clear with a terror sharper than any he'd felt under shellfire, assessed the situation with brutal efficiency. The hollow where he'd found Penny was the only cover. It was a coffin niche, but it was all he had.

He squeezed into it, pressing his back against the cold, wet clay, pulling his knees up to his chest. He was a man trying to become part of the wall, to erase his own outline. Penny, now a hard lump of tense muscle against his sternum, had gone completely, unnaturally still. The shivering stopped. She understood silence.

He heard the sounds of close-quarters fighting filter down the sap—muffled but horrifically clear. The clash of bayonets meeting, a sound like scraping farm tools. A scream, high and desperate, cut brutally short. More German shouts, this time triumphant. They were in the main trench, just around the corner. Any second, one of them could glance down this dark alley, decide to clear it.

Then, a new sound. Boots. Splashing, heavy, purposeful boots. Coming closer. Coming *down the sap*.

Tommy's blood turned to ice slurry in his veins. He held his breath until spots danced before his eyes. The rifle was across his lap, utterly useless. To move it was to be seen. To breathe too loudly was to be heard. He closed his eyes, as if that could make him invisible, a child's superstition he embraced with the fervour of a dying man.

The boots stopped just around the bend, not five yards away. He could hear the man's laboured breathing, the wet suck of mud with each slight shift of weight. A muttered curse in German—*"Verdammtes Loch."* The damned hole. The raider was checking the sap, ensuring it was clear of defenders, looking perhaps for a hiding place for himself or a vantage point to fire into the British trench from the flank.

Penny stirred. A tremor ran through her, a precursor to a sound—a meow of protest, a growl of fear. Tommy's hand, under his coat, moved with desperate gentleness. He clamped it gently but firmly over her muzzle, feeling the soft fur of her nose, the sharp points of her little teeth beneath her lips. She went rigid. He could feel the pulse in her tiny jaw hammering against his fingers, a frantic counterpoint to his own stilled heart.

The German took another step. His shadow fell across the wall opposite Tommy's hiding place, thrown by a flare that must have gone up outside. Tommy saw the distorted shape of his coal-scuttle helmet, the long, menacing curve of his rifle barrel. One more step. One more, and he would be looking right at them, a British soldier curled in a hole like a frightened animal.

And then, from the hollow just above Tommy's head, from the darkness behind the collapsed timber where the earth had fallen in, came a sound. A dry, scrabbling, frantic *scritch-scritch-scratch*. Then a high-pitched, angry squeal.

A rat. A big one, its own sanctuary disturbed by the commotion, the vibrations, the scent of human fear. It was making a bid for freedom, scrambling through its own tunnel in the earth.

The German soldier grunted, startled. He took a half-step back, his attention yanked upwards towards the noise in the darkness above. Tommy saw his shadow shift as he looked up, rifle rising slightly. It was a distraction of only two, maybe three seconds. A shift of focus from the dark hollow at eye level to the darkness above.

But it was enough.

From the main trench came a furious, concentrated

burst of British rifle fire, followed by Sergeant Mackay's roar, raw and powerful. "Counter-attack! Push 'em back, lads! Forwards!"

The German in the sap cursed again, louder this time —"*Scheiße!*" His mission was reconnaissance and disruption, not getting pinned in a side-alley by a resurgent defense. The sound of the rat forgotten, he turned and splashed hurriedly back the way he'd come, joining what sounded like the retreat of his raiding party under a sudden, violent surge of British fire.

The sounds of combat receded, moving back across no-man's land, punctuated by the odd final shot, a last, defiant grenade blast. An eerie, trembling quiet returned to the sap, broken only by the eternal drip of water and Tommy's own shaky, explosive exhale. He realized he'd been biting his lower lip hard enough to draw blood.

Slowly, he loosened his grip on Penny's muzzle. She didn't move. He carefully peeled back the flap of his greatcoat.

Two green eyes stared up at him. They were no longer wide with blind, animal fear. They were sharp, knowing, intense. She had felt the hammer of his heart against her. She had heard the enemy's boots, his foreign curses. She had understood the terrible silence that followed, and what it meant. She gave a small, quiet *mrrp,* a sound that was neither thanks nor forgiveness, but an acknowledgment. A statement: *I am here. You are here. We are alive.* A truce, reforged not in comfort, but in shared terror in the dark.

Slowly, stiffly, as if his joints had rusted, Tommy unfolded himself from the hollow. Every muscle ached with tension. He tucked Penny more securely inside his coat, where she settled after a moment, not as a trembling fugitive, but as a familiar weight. A warm, living weight against the chill that had settled deep in his bones.

He emerged from the sap into the main trench. It was a scene of controlled chaos under the flickering light of dying flares. Wounded were being tended by stretcher-bearers with red cross brassards. Men were assessing damage, piling new sandbags where the parapet had been blown in. Spent cartridges littered the duckboards like brass confetti. The air stank of blood, cordite, and the peculiar, acrid smell of high explosives.

Sergeant Mackay saw him and strode over, his face like thunder under the rim of his helmet. "Finch! Where in blazes have you been? I needed every man on that counter-push!" Spittle flew from his lips.

Tommy stood straight, his mind blank of any excuse that would make sense in this world of mud and death. "Checking the forward sap, Sarge," he said, his voice surprisingly steady. "Thought I heard movement."

Mackay's eyes—hard, experienced chips of flint—narrowed. They scanned him, taking in the fresh mud, the pallor beneath the grime, the way one hand was pressed protectively against his chest, holding the greatcoat closed. His gaze dropped. A single, muddy ginger paw was visible where Tommy's coat gaped open, hooked over the edge of the wool.

Mackay stared at that paw for a long, silent second. The paw, as if sensing the scrutiny, retracted slowly, disappearing back into the dark interior.

The Sergeant's severe expression didn't change, not a twitch. But something in his eyes shifted. The fury banked, replaced by a weary, profound understanding. He'd seen the cat bolt. He'd seen Finch go after it, against all orders, against all sense. He'd also just won a frantic, bloody close-quarters fight with surprisingly minimal losses. And now here was Finch, back from the dead-end sap with his cat and a story about 'movement.'

"Movement, eh?" Mackay said, his voice gravelly. "And?"

"All clear now, Sarge," Tommy said, meeting his gaze. "Just a rat."

Mackay held his gaze for a moment longer, then grunted. It was a sound of acceptance, of a line being drawn under an incident that would not be recorded in any report.

"See that it is. Now get yourself to the dugout. Clean that muck off. And for God's sake," he added, turning away, "keep that creature under control. We've a war to fight, not a menagerie to manage."

"Yes, Sarge."

As Tommy turned to go, weaving through the tired, busy men, he felt it. A vibration against his chest, through the wool and cotton. Soft at first, then growing. Tentative, almost inaudible beneath the distant guns and the sergeants' shouts and the moans of the wounded.

Purring.

He walked back through the trench, past men cleaning their rifles with mechanical motions, past others binding wounds with clumsy, bloody hands. A faint, unthinkable smile touched his cracked, muddy lips, so foreign a sensation he barely recognized it. In his coat, a cat purred. In the sap, a rat had scurried. And in the space between the enemy's boot and the bayonet, he was still alive.

It wasn't glory. It wasn't heroism. It was something simpler, and in this place, far more valuable.

It was, against all odds, a pennyworth of luck.

Chapter 4
The Trench Queen

WINTER CLAMPED ITS iron fist upon the Salient, and the world shrank to the dimensions of a frozen ditch. The rain, which had been a constant, weeping companion, ceased its liquid torture only to be replaced by a more insidious enemy. First came sleet, needling and horizontal, driven by winds that howled down from the North Sea with nothing to stop them but the broken teeth of the Flanders landscape. Then the snow—not the picturesque blanket of Christmas cards, but a thin, gritty shroud that fell for days, bleaching the colour from an already monochrome world. It did nothing to cleanse; it only concealed, turning shell holes into treacherous white traps, burying the dead in anonymous mounds, and making the mud beneath a frozen, jagged nightmare.

The cold was worse than any sniper. A sniper you could theoretically avoid. The cold was everywhere. It crept through layers of wool and leather, settled in the bones with a damp, aching permanence, and turned sentry duty into a trembling, teeth-chattering agony where a man's greatest fear wasn't the enemy, but falling asleep and freezing to death on his feet. Men's breath froze on their scarves, forming icy masks. Fingers turned white and clumsy around rifle bolts. The rum ration, issued each evening, became a medicinal necessity, a bolt of fire in the gut that did little to warm the extremities.

Penny's world contracted to a radius of twenty yards

from the glowing, sacred heart of the dugout's brazier. Her great hunts into no-man's land ceased entirely. The empire of the rats was now too far, too cold, too deadly. Her kingdom became the dark, earthy cavern shared with ten increasingly haggard men, its borders marked by the frozen firestep at one end and the reeking, ice-rimmed latrine at the other. Her title, unofficially bestowed by Alfie during a game of Housey-Housey (Bingo), was "Trench Queen," and she ruled with a paw of iron wrapped in ginger fur.

Her routine was regal and unvarying, a liturgy of survival. Mornings were spent on Tommy's bunk, a warm, ginger loaf soaking up the residual heat from his body, her chin resting on his pack. Afternoons saw her holding court by the brazier, the focal point of all life in the dugout. Here she accepted tribute with a slow blink of her bottle-green eyes—a scrap of precious bacon rind from Alfie, a dab of margarine on a fingertip from young Perkins (who missed his family's cat more than he admitted), a fragment of hard biscuit softened in tea from Sergeant Mackay himself, offered with a gruff, "Don't get used to it."

Her primary duty, rattling, continued with grim, efficient zeal. The rats, also feeling the pinch of winter and growing bolder in their desperation for warmth and food, made incursions into the dugout itself. They met a swift, silent end. Penny's kills were no longer dragged to Tommy as tax payments; they were left as grim ornaments at the dugout entrance, tiny, frozen carcasses arranged with a kind of territorial statement. A warning to others of her kind: *This is my domain.*

Her early-warning system, honed by months at the front, became more nuanced, more vital. The men learned to read her like a barometer, her body a more reliable instrument than any issued by the Meteorological Office.

"Penny's got that look," Perkins would whisper, watching the cat sit statue-still on an ammunition box, her tail tip twitching with the metronomic precision of a mad clock. Minutes later, the first distant *crump* of a ranging shot would echo across the lines, the prelude to a harassing fire.

When she abruptly stopped washing, her head cocked at an odd angle as if listening to a conversation in another room, it often meant a working party in no-man's land, the vibrations of their shovels carried through the frozen earth.

But her most celebrated service came one evening in late January. The men were eating a watery stew that was mostly turnip, the air thick with the smell of damp wool and Woodbines. Penny, who had been dozing in her customary spot by Tommy's feet, suddenly leapt up as if stung. She sneezed violently—a sharp, un-catlike *achoo!* —shook her head as if trying to dislodge something, then began batting frantically at her own nose with a paw, her face a picture of profound, offended outrage. She let out a sharp, distressed yowl that cut through the murmur of conversation and shot towards the back of the dugout, where she began scratching urgently at the heavy gas curtain that hung over the entrance.

For a second, there was silence. Then Sergeant Mackay's spoon clattered to the floor. "GAS!" he roared, the word a physical blow in the confined space. "MASKS! NOW!"

The practiced drill, performed in countless training sessions and a few terrifying realities, took over. Within seconds, the world turned to a blur of rubber and glass, the familiar faces of mates becoming grotesque, snouted insects. They had the masks on, the strange, chemical smell of the filter filling their nostrils, before the first mournful wail of the gas alarm rattlers began down the line. Then they heard it: the tell-tale *plop-plop-plop* of canisters landing in no-man's land, like rotten fruit falling.

They waited, a tableau of silent, bug-eyed monsters, listening to the deadly phosgene cloud creep towards their parapet on the night wind. It found a trench already sealed, men already protected. Penny, her own face buried in the crook of Tommy's elbow where he'd tucked her inside his greatcoat, continued to sneeze indignantly against the lingering chemical smell on his uniform, her small body trembling with the insult to her sensitive nose.

When the all-clear sounded an hour later, and they peeled off the stifling masks, the first thing Tommy saw was Penny giving her paws a final, disgusted wipe over her ears, as if trying to erase the entire experience.

After that, her status was unassailable. She was no longer just a ratter or a mascot; she was a life-saving piece of kit. Lieutenant Chambers, who had developed a surreptitious habit of saving the toughest, gristliest bits of his tinned beef for her (claiming he "couldn't stomach them"), formally rescinded his "no animals in the officer's quarters" rule. He declared in a moment of unguarded sentiment after the gas incident, his voice still hoarse from the mask, "That creature is a vital piece of defensive apparatus. As important as a periscope or a wire-cutter." It was the highest praise she would ever receive from the commissioned ranks.

But the cold was the true, grinding enemy. Rations grew scarcer as supply lines faltered in the frozen muck. The sardines became a memory, then a legend. Penny's winter coat grew luxuriously thick, a ruff of fur around her neck that made her look like a miniature, ferocious lion, but her ribs began to show faintly beneath the fluff.

Her energy waned. She spent more time sleeping, a deep, conserving sleep, only rousing for her rattling patrols or when the subtle drop in air pressure signalled an impending shelling.

The worst of it was the quiet. Not the blessed silence of a genuine lull, but the dead, muffled quiet of a world buried and waiting. It pressed down on the men, a weight as physical as the frozen mud on their boots, sapping spirit as the cold sapped strength. Jokes fell flat, dying before they reached their punchlines. Letters from home were read and re-read until the paper wore thin at the folds, the words of love and mundane news offering less comfort each time, becoming a painful reminder of a life that seemed like a fairy tale.

The war wasn't a series of battles anymore; it was an endless, frozen waiting. A cosmic, malevolent boredom punctuated by moments of sheer terror.

It was during this grey, soul-crushing hush that Penny unveiled her final, most unexpected service.

Private Perkins broke. It happened on a night so still and cold they could hear the Germans coughing in their trench two hundred yards away, a sound both eerily intimate and infinitely distant. The strain, the cold, the relentless nothingness—it didn't snap something loudly inside the boy. It dissolved it, quietly, like sugar in cold tea.

He didn't scream or cry. He simply sat on his bunk after evening stand-to, staring at the damp clay wall opposite, shivering violently though he was close to the brazier. Then he began whispering, so low at first Tommy thought he was praying. But the words, repeated over and over, were: "Mum... I want to come home, Mum... please, Mum..."

The men in the dugout shifted uncomfortably, avoiding

each other's eyes. They'd seen this before. It was the prelude to a breakdown, to a trip to the Casualty Clearing Station that might end with a diagnosis of "shell shock" and a ticket to a hospital in Blighty, or, worse, with an unsympathetic officer's verdict of 'cowardice in the face of the enemy' and a firing squad at dawn.

Sergeant Mackay watched from the doorway, his face grim, knowing any harsh word, any attempt to "snap him out of it," might be the push that sent the lad over the edge into screaming, irreversible madness.

Penny, disturbed from her sleep on Tommy's bunk by the change in the emotional weather, hopped down. She picked her way with fastidious care across the muddy, littered floor, past the silent, helpless men, and jumped up onto the bunk beside Perkins. He didn't seem to notice her, his eyes fixed on the wall, his whispers continuing in a desperate loop.

She head-butted his limp, dangling hand. No response. She butted it again, harder. When that elicited nothing, she did something Tommy had never seen her do with anyone, not even him. She climbed deliberately into Perkins's lap.

It was a slow, careful manoeuvre. She kneaded his thin, grey blanket with her paws, turning three precise circles as if carving out a nest. Then she settled down, a perfect circle of warmth on his frozen legs.

And then, she began to purr.

It wasn't her usual, faint rumble of contentment. This was a loud, robust, diesel-engine purr, a vibration that seemed to emanate from the very centre of her being and fill the still, heavy air of the dugout. It was a sound utterly, defiantly *alive*. It cut through the whisper of madness like a knife through fog.

Perkins's whispering stopped. He looked down, his

The Trench Cat of Ypres

eyes bewildered, as if noticing the cat in his lap for the first time. Slowly, tentatively, as if moving through glue, his hand came up. He placed it on Penny's back. The purr intensified, deepening into a palpable thrum. He buried his fingers in her thick ginger fur, feeling the powerful vibration travel up his arm, into his chest. A single, choked sob escaped him, a release of pressure. Then he was quiet, his whole being focused on the simple, solid, animal reality of the purring cat. The warm weight. The relentless, comforting rhythm of life continuing.

No one spoke. The men just watched, their own breathing easing. The terrible, frozen tension in the dugout—the fear that Perkins's crack would spread to them all—began to thaw, molecule by molecule, melted by that mundane, miraculous sound. It was a sound from another world—a world of hearths and knitted blankets and contented creatures by the fire. It was a lifeline thrown across the chasm of despair.

After a full ten minutes, her duty done, Penny stood, stretched with an arch of her back that popped her joints, and jumped lightly down. She returned to Tommy's bunk, leaving behind a boy who, while not healed, was no longer broken. He wiped his face roughly on his sleeve, took a shuddering breath, and gave the men a shaky, embarrassed nod. The spell was broken. The immediate crisis had passed.

Later, in the profound darkness of the dugout when only the glow of the banked brazier and the occasional red dot of a cigarette marked the presence of men, Alfie whispered across the narrow space to Tommy.

"That cat of yours, Tom."

Tommy, listening to Penny's soft, even breathing beside his head, murmured back, "What about her?"

"She's not just a ratter, is she?"

Tommy thought of the gas warning, of the shared terror in the sap, of the purr that had pulled Perkins back from the edge. "No," he said quietly into the dark. "Reckon she's a bit of everything. Sentinel, nurse, artillery spotter... and a queen."

The Trench Queen held her court through the deepest dark of the year. She gave them warnings that kept their bodies alive. She gave them a focus, something outside themselves to care for, that kept their souls from withering. And on the darkest nights, when the cold and the silence threatened to swallow them whole, she gave them a sound that spoke of life persisting, of warmth existing, of a heartbeat continuing against all odds.

She asked for nothing but a little warmth and the odd scrap. And in return, in that frozen, stinking ditch at the ragged edge of the world, she gave them back, piece by fragile piece, a sliver of their humanity. It wasn't heroism. It was quieter, and perhaps because of that, more profound. It was companionship, in its most basic, unadorned, essential form. A small, ginger flame in the long, frozen night.

The thaw, when it came in a fitful, grudging fashion in late March, was a greasy, foul affair. It unlocked a hundred buried smells—the sweet-rotten odour of death and decay held captive by the frost, the sulphurous stink of old explosives, the flat, metallic scent of rusting metal. But with the oozing mud came a change in the air, a shifting of the wind that carried not just new stenches, but new sounds: the distant clank of tracks, the increased drone of observation planes, the bustle of greater activity behind the lines.

Plans were whispered. The word "offensive," dormant all winter, was breathed again in officers' dugouts and around braziers. The great, sleeping war was stretching its limbs, cracking the ice from its joints.

And Penny, sensing the change in the very earth and in the tautness of the men around her, grew restless. She spent long periods on the firestep, no longer just a sleepy sentinel, but an alert surveyor. She stared out at the still-desolate but softening landscape of no-man's land, her tail twitching not with boredom, but with a focused agitation. She was listening to a new set of rumours, ones carried not in the air, but in the vibrations of the ground, in the scent of fresh troops and new machinery, in the electric tension that crackled between the lines.

The waiting was coming to an end. Something vast and terrible was brewing. And the Trench Queen, in her small, fierce, inscrutable way, was preparing her subjects—the ten weary men in her muddy realm—for the storm to come.

Chapter 5
The Calm Before

THE THAW WAS a betrayal. The pristine white shroud, which had at least lent a kind of stark, clean lie to the landscape, melted into a clinging, chocolate-brown morass worse than anything they'd known before. It wasn't mud anymore; it was a substance with sentient malevolence. It sucked at boots with a wet, hungry kiss, claiming them forever. It climbed trouser legs, coated equipment, and seeped into food, tins, and souls with impartial insistence.

This melt unlocked the frozen secrets of the winter: the rusted tang of old iron from a thousand shattered guns, the sweet-sickly smell of things long buried now rising in gaseous bubbles from crater pools, and a plague of insects that hatched in the sudden, deceptive warmth, rising in humming, vindictive clouds from stagnant water. Flies, born on the dead, found the living.

But with the mud came a strange, tense energy, a current that ran through the trench like a low-voltage wire. The air itself seemed charged, thick with unspoken orders, the clatter of renewed activity, and the constant, distant rumble of lorries moving up by night along the camouflaged *pavé* roads behind the lines. The feeling was palpable—the war was winding a spring, tightening a screw.

Penny felt it first. Her winter restlessness evolved into a low-grade, perpetual vigilance. She abandoned her throne by the brazier, which now burned less often as coal grew scarce, for higher ground. She took to the firestep, the roof of a dugout (to Sergeant Mackay's irritation), or a pile of ammunition boxes stacked in a traverse. She would sit for hours, a ginger sentinel outlined against the grey sky, her ears performing slow, continuous sweeps like radar dishes. She tracked not just the returning birds—starlings and crows that wheeled over the shattered trees—but the deeper, more menacing sounds: the metallic *clank-clank* of tank tracks being unloaded from flatcars miles back, the increased, buzzing frequency of RE8 reconnaissance planes droning high above like malignant dragonflies, the distant, earth-shaking *thump* of artillery being moved into new, forward positions.

Her warnings changed. No longer just for immediate shelling or gas, they became more generalized, more ominous. A low, troubled growl lodged in her throat might signal not an incoming round, but the passage of a large troop movement in the German trenches opposite, sensed through minute vibrations in the earth transmitted along the chalk and clay. She began to avoid certain sections of their own trench, slinking past with her belly low to the duckboards, her fur slightly on end, as if the very ground there was tainted, cursed. The men, superstitious by nature and now hyper-attuned to her every nuance, began to avoid those spots too. They called them "Penny's patches," and a rumour spread that a man hit by a sniper in traverse D had been standing on one just that morning.

Lieutenant Chambers, now gaunt with shadows like bruises under his eyes and a permanent, fine tremor in his hands that had nothing to do with the cold, called it "feline intuition" in a report to Battalion HQ. Sergeant

Mackay, reading over his shoulder, had grunted, "Call it what you like, sir. That cat knows more than the brass do." Tommy just watched her, a knot of cold dread tightening in his stomach each time he saw her tense pose. Her intelligence was no longer a comfort; it was a confirmation. The storm wasn't just coming; it was building to a fury, and she could feel its atmospheric pressure dropping.

Rations improved slightly, a sinister form of fattening. Tins of oily Machonochie stew with actual chunks of meat appeared. The hardtack biscuits came with less weevil. There was a rare, glorious issue of plum-and-apple jam, "Tickler's," that tasted like heaven on the grey bread. It was the army preparing the lamb, giving it one last good meal.

New faces appeared in the trench, fresh replacements for the winter's silent losses to flu, frostbite, and sniper's bullets. They were painfully young, pink-cheeked beneath their new, stiff khaki, wide-eyed with a mixture of awe at the veterans and terror of the landscape. They looked at the caked, weary men of the section as if they were creatures from another planet, and at Penny with simple, uncomplicated curiosity.

"Cor, a cat!" one of them, a boy named Davies from the Welsh valleys, exclaimed on his first day. He reached out a tentative hand to pet her as she sat regally on a sandbag, cleaning a paw.

Penny paused her ablutions. She fixed him with a withering, emerald stare that seemed to take in his cleanliness, his nervousness, his entire unblooded existence. Then she delivered a swift, warning bat with a sheathed paw, a *thump* on the back of his hand that was more insult than injury.

Davies snatched his hand back as if burned, his face

The Trench Cat of Ypres

flushing. The veterans—Alfie, Johnson, the others—let out a dry, rasping chorus of laughter that held no joy, only a grim satisfaction.

"She ain't a pet, son," Alfie said, lighting a cigarette with a cupped hand. "She's more like... the foreman. You mind her, she minds you. You don't..." He blew out a plume of smoke. "Well, you saw."

The men spent their days in a frenzy of activity that felt both urgent and utterly futile. They repaired duckboards that sank into the mire overnight. They strengthened parapets with new sandbags that were immediately shot to rags. They strung new, glistening coils of barbed wire in front of their line—thick, cruel stuff that promised a horrible, tangled death to anyone trying to cross it. They were, Tommy thought with a cold clarity, building their own cage, reinforcing the bars of the prison they were about to be ordered to break out of.

Through it all, Penny watched, her green eyes missing nothing, her tail twitching with a rhythmic anxiety.

One evening, a new sound joined the familiar symphony of war: a deep, subterranean *thump*, felt more in the soles of the feet and the pit of the stomach than heard. Then another, closer. A faint tremor ran through the tea in their mugs, concentric circles vibrating on the brown surface.

"Mining," Sergeant Mackay said, his voice flat. He didn't look up from the letter he was writing. "Ours or theirs, God knows. They're planting bloody great seeds down there."

The world was becoming dangerous from every direction: from above with shells and gas, from the sides with snipers and raiders, and now from below, where men fought like monstrous moles in the dark, planting tons of ammonal to blow each other sky-high from beneath.

Penny vanished for a full day after the first major underground blast shook their section of the line—a British mine under a German listening post that sent a fountain of earth and timber two hundred feet into the air. Tommy searched, the old, familiar panic rising in his throat, but it was useless in the crowded, chaotic trench. She returned at dusk, slinking along the parapet, her fur matted with a different kind of mud—chalky, pale, and dry, the dust of deep earth. She had, it seemed, been investigating this new, unseen layer of the war. She refused the food Tommy offered, drank deeply from a rusty puddle, then crawled into her crate and slept for sixteen hours straight, a sleep of such profound exhaustion it looked like a small, furry coma.

The final sign came on a clear, breezy day in early April. The artillery, which had been trading desultory, harassing fire for weeks, fell completely, utterly silent. Not a single field gun, not a lone mortar, not a spiteful whizz-bang. The silence was profound, unnerving, heavier than any barrage. It was a vacuum that sucked at the ears. Birds sang with shocking clarity in the rusted wire. Men spoke in hushed tones, as if in a cathedral or a sickroom, waiting for the last breath.

Penny, on the firestep, did not relax into this silence. She became hyper-alert, a coil of tense muscle and nerve. She paced a short, tight path—three steps one way, three steps back—her tail puffed to twice its normal size, a bristling bottlebrush. She would stare fixedly at a point on the German line for minutes on end, then swivel with abrupt, mechanical precision to stare at their own support trenches behind them, then up at the empty, innocent blue sky. She was connecting dots invisible to them, tracing the pattern of the coming storm in the stillness.

Tommy found her like that, a bundle of vibrating tension. He sat beside her on the firestep, not touching her, sharing the watch. "What is it, girl?" he murmured, the sound too small in the vast quiet. "What can you hear?"

She looked at him, and for a fleeting second, her regal aloofness vanished. In her wide, green eyes, he saw a reflection of his own fear—sharp, undiluted, animal. It was a moment of pure, wordless understanding between species: *I am afraid. You are afraid. It is coming.* Then she blinked, the shutters came down, and she went back to her pacing, a tiny engine of dread.

That night, the rumours solidified into hard, cold orders. They were to be relieved before dawn. A fresh battalion—the Leinsters, all Irish accents and new boots—was coming up. Their section was to move back to the support line, then further back to reserve. It was the classic, chilling pre-offensive shuffle. The chess pieces were being rearranged for the great, bloody push.

As they packed their meagre kits—a spare shirt, a toothbrush, letters, a precious photograph—a strange, somber mood settled over the dugout. There was relief, palpable as a sigh, at leaving the front line, the immediate stare of death. But it was poisoned, soured, by the certain knowledge of *why* they were leaving. They were being moved aside to make room. They were the veterans, the survivors, being pulled back so they could be fed into the grinder at the precise moment when the fresh meat had been chewed up and the attack was stalling. They were the spare parts, kept in reserve for the emergency.

Tommy rolled his puttees with automatic, practiced motions. Penny wove between their legs, an anxious, ginger shadow, her usual dignity replaced by a restless confusion. She seemed to understand that the delicate, hard-won ecosystem of her dugout-court—the familiar smells, the assigned sleeping spots, the rhythm of the watches—was about to be violently dismantled.

Sergeant Mackay appeared in the dugout entrance, his face unreadable in the gloom of a single candle. "Right. We move in twenty. Travel light. Weapons, ammunition, greatcoats. The rest stays." His eyes scanned the space, landing on Tommy. "And Finch?"

"Sergeant?"

"See to the cat."

It wasn't an order to bring her. It was an order to *see to her*. To decide her fate. To leave her to the new battalion (who might not appreciate a ginger monarch), to turn her loose in the trench (a death sentence), or to solve the problem more permanently. Mackay's gaze held Tommy's for a second, then moved on. The burden was handed over.

The men filed out into the trench, a line of shadows shuffling towards the communication trench that led to the rear, to the "safe" ground that was only safe until the barrage began. Tommy was last. He looked at Penny, who sat amidst the suddenly empty, gloomy space, surrounded by the discarded junk of their lives: empty tins, a broken pipe, a waterlogged magazine. Her kingdom was abandoned.

He couldn't leave her. He just couldn't. The image of her waiting for a sardine that would never come, watching for familiar faces that had vanished, was more than he could bear. He opened his haversack, the one with the torn strap mended now with rough, gray thread from a kit. "C'mon, Pen," he said, his voice gentle. "New digs. Can't be worse than this, can it?"

She hesitated, looking from him to the dark mouth of

the dugout that had been her home through gas and snow and shelling. Then, with a grace that belied the weight of the moment, she leapt lightly into the open bag. She curled up, making herself a perfect, compact fit, her head poking out the top like a furry periscope. Tommy hoisted the bag onto his back, adjusting the straps. Her weight was familiar, a comforting pressure against his shoulder blades, a living kit.

He joined the end of the line of silent men shuffling through the winding trench. The night was clear, starry, and deceptively peaceful. A half-moon cast sharp shadows. Behind them, the front line they had inhabited and cursed and somehow made a home in for months lay dark and quiet, waiting for its new occupants. Ahead, unseen in the night, thousands of men and hundreds of thousands of shells were gathering, a storm of steel and flesh waiting for the dawn.

In the haversack on his back, Penny was still. But as they moved further from their trench, from the known universe of mud and rat and routine, Tommy felt her head turn. She was looking back. Then, she gave a single, soft sigh, her breath warm and moist against the nape of his neck, and settled down, her chin resting on the bag's edge.

The Trench Queen had abdicated her throne. She was just a cat in a bag now, moving with her man into the unknown dark, towards the great, roaring horror that she, better than any of them with their maps and orders, had already sensed was coming.

The calm was over.

Chapter 6
The Waiting Place

THE SUPPORT TRENCH was a wider, deeper gash in the earth, but it felt more dangerous than the front line's intimate, tense silence. It was a choked artery of the war, pulsing with a frantic, disordered life. Here, the machinery was exposed, stripped of the front line's grim purpose. Ammunition parties laden with heavy boxes jostled past ration carriers struggling with sandbags of bread. Signallers, their faces smeared with black grease, tripped over snaking cables while cursing in inventive Cockney. Harrowed-faced officers with red tabs barked at pale clerks clutching clipboards, demanding status reports that were obsolete before the pencil left the paper. And everywhere, in every niche and dugout alcove, was the low, ceaseless groan of men waiting—a sound as much a part of the trench as the mud.

Penny refused to stay in the haversack. The moment Tommy unshouldered it in the crowded, reeking alcove that was their new, temporary dugout, she sprang out as if ejected. She landed with a soft thud on a crate stenciled with the ominous words "Mills Bombs, No. 5, Handle With Care," surveyed the frantic scene with palpable feline disdain, and vanished into the narrow canyon between two stacks of ration boxes.

"Suit yourself," Tommy muttered, too weary from the march and the weight of anticipation to coax her. The front line, for all its horrors, had had a terrible, stark simplicity: you faced the enemy. This place was all gnawing, undefined dread. It was the antechamber to the abattoir.

Their new dugout was shared with another section from a different company, strangers with the same hollow eyes and permanent stoop. The air was thick and soupy with new smells layered over the old: damp wool, cheap tobacco, the greasy aroma of machined metal from freshly opened ammunition crates, and a new, acrid, sweaty scent—the collective fear of thousands of men, sweating from pores that knew what was coming.

They were in reserve for the "Big Push." The words hung in the air, whispered in every conversation, seen in every glance at the unnaturally quiet eastern sky. It meant they would wait here, in this tumultuous limbo, until the first waves went over the top at Zero Hour. Then they would wait some more, listening to the sounds of battle, trying to decipher its progress from the pitch and fury of the noise. Finally, they would be fed into the machine—where it was faltering, to plug a gap, or where a breakthrough was happening, to exploit it. They were the spare parts, kept in the toolbox until the mechanism broke or screamed for more fuel.

For two days, Penny was a ghost in this new underworld. Tommy caught only glimpses of her—a flicker of ginger tail disappearing around a corner into a sap, a pair of luminous eyes gleaming from a niche high up in a traverse where she'd found a dry perch, the tip of an ear visible behind a pile of empty fuel cans. She was a small, furry cartographer, mapping this noisy, unfamiliar territory, finding its quiet edges and secret pathways.

She was also, Tommy noticed with a troubled frown, hunting with a grim, silent desperation unlike her usual efficient sport. The rats here were different—fewer, but fatter and sleeker, thriving on the rich detritus of a massed army: spilled flour, discarded food tins, the occasional unguarded haversack. Penny left her kills not as territorial ornaments, but hidden—under duckboards, behind crates, in shallow scrapes in the clay. It was the behaviour of a creature storing up, preparing for a famine. It chilled him.

On the third day, she returned to him. He was sitting on an upturned ammunition box, cleaning his rifle for the tenth time that day, the rhythmic *snick-snick* of the pull-through and the smell of Hoppe's No. 9 solvent the only things holding his whirling thoughts at bay. She jumped onto the crate beside him, sat neatly, wrapped her tail around her feet, and began meticulously washing a paw. It was a performance of supreme normalcy, but her ears were perpetually in motion, swivelling to track every shouted order from an NCO, every rumble of a distant lorry grinding up the Menin Road, every barked cough from the trench.

"Seen enough, have you?" Tommy asked softly, not looking at her, focusing on the gleam of the rifle bore.

She paused her washing, one paw held in mid-air, to give him a long, inscrutable look. Her eyes seemed to hold centuries of predator wisdom. Then she resumed, licking between her toes with fierce concentration.

That evening, as a watery sun bled away behind them, the final, deafening pieces of the machinery slotted into place.

It started not with a bang, but with a silence deeper than before. Then, from far behind their lines, from the hidden gun parks and camouflaged emplacements, came a single, massive *CRUMP*. It was so deep it was felt more than heard—a physical pressure in the chest, a shudder in the ground that made the tea in Tommy's mug slop

The Trench Cat of Ypres

over the rim. A gun so large it had its own weather.

Before the echo had died, another joined it. Then another. Not sporadic, not harassing. Methodical. Relentless.

Within an hour, the world dissolved into sound.

This was not the shelling they knew. This was a continuous, roaring avalanche of noise that blotted out all other sensation. The sky to the east, over the German lines, began to flicker with a constant, hellish light—stuttering oranges, blinding whites, and sullen reds that pulsed like a monstrous, diseased heart. The ground trembled incessantly, a low-grade earthquake that made teeth rattle in jaws. The air vibrated, thick with concussion. Men stopped speaking because it was pointless; they communicated with gestures, with taps on the shoulder, with wide, white-rimmed eyes.

The men in the support trench didn't cheer. They huddled lower in their funk holes, some clamping hands over their ears, others simply staring at the vibrating earth between their boots. This was the overture. This was the industrial hammer, meant to smash the anvil flat before they, the human metal, were thrown upon it.

And Penny... Penny went mad.

The carefully maintained façade of regal composure, the aloof dignity she had carried through gas attacks and shellings, shattered into a million pieces. She let out a shriek that cut through even the all-consuming roar—a sound of pure, elemental, sanity-breaking terror. It was the cry of a creature whose entire sensory world, its primary means of navigating reality, had been turned into a solid wall of agony.

She bolted. Not into a hidey-hole, but in frantic, useless circles in the confined, crowded space of the dugout. She became a ginger pinball of panic, bouncing off the clay walls, scrambling over men's legs, ricocheting from a stack of blankets to a crate of grenades. Her claws snagged on wool, on canvas, on Tommy's hand as he lunged to grab her, drawing thin, stinging lines of blood.

"Bloody hell, control that thing!" shouted a corporal from the other section, a big man with a broken nose, flinching as she shot between his legs.

Tommy tried again, but she was a blur, all fear and flying fur. The world of sound she had always warned them about, had always given them precious seconds to prepare for, had now expanded to engulf the entire universe. There was no 'away.' There was no safe cranny. Her early-warning system was useless, obsolete; the danger was everywhere, inescapable, a physical pressure on her eardrums, a vibration in her whiskers, a terror in her bones.

Finally, with a last desperate scramble, she shot into Tommy's open haversack which lay at his feet. She burrowed deep, past his spare socks, his mess tin, to the very bottom where an empty bully beef tin lay. She curled into a tight, trembling ball around it, as if its familiar, meaty scent was the last anchor in the world, and did not move.

Tommy, his hand stinging, slowly closed the flap of the haversack partway, leaving a gap for air. He could feel her shivering through the thick canvas, a high-frequency vibration against his leg when he touched the bag. He remembered her in the sap, frozen by the terror of a single shell. This was that, multiplied by a thousand, by a million. This was the end of the world, in sound.

The bombardment went on all night. An eternity in hell. No one slept. They sat in the shaking, shuddering earth, coated in a fine, persistent dust shaken from the roof with each nearby impact. Their faces were lit by the distant, constant flashes—one after another after another, a stroboscopic nightmare that burned onto the retina. The sound was so immense, so total, it became a kind of silence itself—a deafening white noise that swallowed thought, swallowed time, swallowed everything but the primal need for it to stop.

Just before a grey, filthy dawn, it did.

The silence that followed was more shocking, more violent, than the noise had been. It was a ringing, vacuum silence, heavy and absolute. Men winced, clutched their ears, opened and closed their mouths to pop them. Tommy's own ears buzzed painfully, filled with a high-pitched whine like a dying mosquito. The absence of pressure was a pressure in itself.

In the haversack between his feet, the frantic trembling stopped. There was a cautious shift of weight, a slow uncurling.

Then, from the east, carried on a dawn wind that now smelled only of cordite and scorched earth, came a new sound. Faint at first, then growing, spreading along the line like a contagion. Not guns. Not explosions.

A high, thin, ululating cry, made by thousands of human voices, tinny and desperate through whistles.

The infantry were going over the top.

The Big Push had begun.

Sergeant Mackay appeared at the dugout entrance, his face the colour of wood ash, his eyes red-raw. He looked a hundred years old. "Stand to," he said, his voice a raspy ruin from the dust and the night. It wasn't an order; it was a statement of inevitable fact. "Make ready. We move when ordered."

The waiting was over. Now came the waiting to be used.

With movements that felt thick and dreamlike, Tommy

stood. He shouldered his rifle, adjusted the straps of his small pack, then lifted the haversack. He felt Penny adjust inside, a small, warm, living weight settling against the small of his back. She wasn't hiding from the silence anymore; she was bracing for what came next. The blind, brainless panic was gone, burned away by the long night. What was left in the tense set of her body he could feel through the canvas was a dreadful, shared understanding. A resignation. They were in it now, all the way.

They filed out into the trench. The sky was lightening to a dirty, streaked grey, like water used to wash a paintbrush. The air stank of spent energy—cordite, burnt powder, and something else, something coppery and sweet that hadn't been there before. Men moved like automatons, checking and re-checking their rifles with hands that shook not from the cold but from a surfeit of adrenaline. They fixed bayonets with a soft, deadly *snick* of metal on metal. They didn't speak. There was nothing to say. They just listened, their heads cocked, to the new symphony that had replaced the bombardment: the distant, frantic rattle of machine-gun fire—German Maxim guns, by the sound, like monstrous, tearing canvas. The sharper *pop-pop-pop* of British Lewis guns answering. The isolated *crack* of sniper rifles. And underneath it all, that terrible moaning haze, which was not the wind.

Tommy leaned against the cold, damp clay of the trench wall, feeling the gentle, restless movement in the bag on his back. He closed his eyes for a second, not to sleep, but to remember. He thought of Penny's winter kingdom—the quiet dugout, the glow of the brazier on her fur, the predictable, almost comforting scuttle of rats in the walls, the soft purr in the dark. That small, contained world was gone, blasted into atoms by the night's economy-sized storm of iron.

Alfie materialised beside him as if conjured from the mist, offering a cigarette. Tommy took it, let Alfie light it with a cupped match. The smoke was harsh in his raw, dust-lined throat, but it was a sensation, a point of focus.

"Reckon she knows?" Alfie asked quietly, nodding towards the haversack with his chin. His face was grim.

"Yeah," Tommy said, exhaling a thin, blue plume into the cold, foul air. "She knows."

"What's she doing in there?"

Tommy listened. Beneath the growing cacophony from the east, beneath the shuffling and muttering in the trench, he could just make it out. A low, steady, rhythmic vibration transmitted through the canvas and into his spine.

"She's purring."

Alfie stared at him, his eyes blank for a second. Then his face contorted, and he let out a short, shocked bark of laughter that held no humour at all, just a kind of dizzying incredulity. "Purring? *Now?*"

Tommy just nodded, taking another drag. It wasn't the contented rumble of a cat by a hearth. It was the purr of a creature in the jaws of extreme stress—a self-soothing mechanism wired deep into its biology, a tiny, stubborn engine of life humming defiantly in the face of the vast, impersonal machine of death grinding into motion over the ridge. In that moment, it seemed to Tommy the bravest, loneliest, most heartbreaking sound in the world.

The order came down the line, passed from mouth to ear in a grim, quick whisper that slithered along the trench like a snake.

Forward. Prep to advance.

The spare parts were being called for. The machine was jamming, and their piece was needed.

Tommy took one last, deep drag on the cigarette, then stamped it into the mud with his heel. He adjusted the straps of his haversack one final time. The purring vibrated against his spine, a constant, fragile thread of warmth in the creeping chill.

"Right then, Pen," he whispered, so low only she, pressed against his back, could possibly hear. "Let's go and see what's what."

And with that, he moved forward into the stream of men, towards the communication trench that led not to safety, but to the roaring, smoking east.

Chapter 7
The Great Absence

THEY MOVED FORWARD not in a heroic, bayonet-waving rush, but in a grim, trudging shuffle. They were a river of mud-coloured men flowing up the choked communication trenches towards the thunder, against the current of stretcher-bearers coming the other way. The bearers' faces were fixed, their eyes looking at nothing as they navigated the narrow boards with their groaning, dripping burdens. The two streams passed in silence, the advancing men careful not to look too closely at what was being carried past, the bearers focused on not jostling their cargo.

The sound ahead was different now. Less the monolithic, world-hammering roar of the bombardment, more a ragged, discordant symphony of violence in its active phase. The staccato, ripping-cloth sound of German Maxim guns. The slower, deeper *chug-chug-chug* of British Vickers guns answering. The spiteful *crack* of sniper rifles, hunting for officers and machine-gun crews. The crump of mortar bombs walking across the torn earth. And underneath it all, woven through the mechanical noises, was a terrible, human sound—not screams exactly, but a low, constant moaning haze, punctuated by sharp cries. It was the sound of the battle breathing.

The air thickened with new smells that clung to the back of the throat, a layered cocktail of destruction: the sharp, bitter reek of cordite, the greasy smoke from burning oil or flesh, the damp-earth smell of fresh craters, and something else, a sweet-rotten undertone that made Tommy's stomach clench. *That* smell, he knew from Passchendaele, was the smell of the ground opening up its secrets.

Penny, in the haversack, had gone utterly, unnaturally still. Not the stillness of sleep, but the absolute frozen stillness of a prey animal that knows any movement is death.

They reached what had been the British front line. It was unrecognisable, a place out of a fever-dream. The neat parapets, the tidy firesteps, the carefully maintained fields of fire—all gone. In their place was a chaotic, smoking wasteland of craters that overlapped like bubbles in a pot of boiling mud. Some were so vast and deep they had lakes of filthy, rainbow-slicked water at the bottom. The German wire, which the great bombardment was meant to have vaporized, hung in shredded, greasy clumps from splintered posts, still lethal. And in the wire, in the craters, sprawled across the lips of what used to be trenches, were the men.

The first wave. Some moved—a twitching hand, a leg dragging a meaningless furrow in the mud. Most did not. They lay in the grotesquely graceful poses of the suddenly emptied, their bright new uniforms, put on for the Big Push, already the colour of the earth, soaked in it. Here and there, a patch of pale skin, a shock of hair, a hand clutching a photograph, stood out with shocking clarity. This was the work of the first hour. The war had harvested its initial crop, and it lay scattered across the field.

Their orders, passed by a panting, wild-eyed runner, were to reinforce a reported "incursion" in the second

The Trench Cat of Ypres

German line. Sergeant Mackay, his face now a stone mask under his helmet, gave no speech. He simply pointed with his bayonet towards the east, towards the source of the Maxim gun's chatter, and led them up and over the debris of their own parapet, into the geometric nightmare of no-man's land.

Here, the world lost all horizon, all sense of up or down. It was a swirling, grey-brown chaos of smoke, flying clods of earth, and the whistle and whine of metal cutting the air. Men ran in short, crouching bursts from crater to crater. Others lay where they had fallen, becoming part of the landscape. Orders were screamed and lost in the din.

Tommy kept his eyes locked on the back of Alfie's pack, a square of fading khaki in the murk. His world narrowed to the next shell hole, the next stumbling step, the next gulp of foul air. The weight on his back was forgotten, absorbed into the greater, all-consuming weight of the fear that pressed on him from all sides.

They plunged, one by one, into a captured German trench. It felt alien, wrong. It was shallower, dug with different angles, the firing steps on the opposite side. The smell was different too—a harsher tobacco, a different kind of disinfectant. And it was full of the dead. Men in field-grey lay tangled with men in khaki, frozen in a final, intimate struggle or collapsed separately, killed by the same shell or grenade. The fighting had moved on, a wave that had washed through this section and receded, leaving this bloody, tangled flotsam behind.

"Here! Dig in here! Johnson, cover that traverse! Finch, on the parapet, watch for counter-attack from the left!" Mackay's voice was a raw scrape, but it cut through the fog in Tommy's head.

They dropped into the filth of the foreign trench,

slamming their bodies against the chalky, unfamiliar earth. Tommy scrambled into a shallow funk hole, pulling his rifle to his shoulder, peering through a gap in the sandbags into the swirling smoke of no-man's land beyond. Alfie slumped into the hole beside him, breathing in great, ragged gulps that were half-sobs.

It was then Tommy felt the movement. A violent, desperate thrashing in the haversack, still slung on his back. He'd forgotten her entirely. The world had shrunk to the circle of his rifle sights.

He cursed, fumbling behind him with one hand for the buckle, his eyes still scanning the smoke. He got it open.

Penny exploded out as if launched from a cannon. She hit the trench bottom with a soft thud, slipped in the bloody mud, righted herself. For a second, she stood there, utterly disoriented. Then it all hit her—the concentrated, close-quarter sounds (so much louder here), the overwhelming, choking smells of blood, excrement, and death, the vibrations of nearby impacts. It was an assault a thousand times more intimate and horrifying than the distant bombardment in the support trench. That had been noise. This was the source. This was the raw, screaming, stinking heart of it.

Her fur stood on end, transforming her into a bristling, orange puffball. Her back arched, her tail thickened. She opened her mouth in a silent, wide hiss at the world, at the torn earth, at the sky, at everything.

"Penny!" Tommy hissed, making a frantic grab for her.

But she was gone. She streaked down the trench, a blur of ginger terror, slipping and skidding, disappearing around a corner where the smoke from a burning ammunition box hung thick and acrid.

"Leave it, Finch!" Mackay snarled from a few yards away, his rifle trained on the parapet. "Jerry counter-

The Trench Cat of Ypres

attack could come any second! Keep your eyes front!"

Tommy stared after her, a hollow, cold space opening up beneath his ribs. This was different from her bolting in the sap, or even during the barrage. That was fear of a specific thing. This was a flight from reality itself, into a landscape designed to kill everything in it. He saw in his mind's eye what would find her: a shell blast turning her to red mist, a stray bullet, a falling, crushing body from a parapet. Or simply the overwhelming, senseless terror of it all, freezing her in the open until a boot or a bayonet found her.

But Mackay was right. To go after her now was suicide, and a betrayal of the men beside him who depended on him watching their flank. It was dereliction. With a feeling like tearing his own skin, he turned back to the parapet, his throat so tight he couldn't swallow. The absence at his back, where her warm weight and soft purr had been, felt heavier, more profound, than her physical weight ever had. It was a void.

The expected German counter-attack came twenty minutes later, not in a massed charge, but in a whirlwind of movement and noise. Stick grenades arced over the parapet with their distinctive, fluttering sound. Shouts of *"Vorwärts!"* Guttural, close. It was brief, brutal, and personal. It was driven back by a blistering, disciplined volley of rifle fire from Mackay's men and the sustained, angry chatter of a Lewis gun that Johnson had set up in a traverse, spitting brass into the mud.

When it was over, the trench smelled of blood and burnt powder and the sour tang of released adrenaline. Two more of their section were down—one silent, one crying softly for his mother. And in the sudden, comparative lull, Tommy couldn't help himself.

"Sarge." His voice was a croak. "The cat."

Mackay, checking the breech of his rifle, looked at him. Then his gaze swept over the hellscape of the captured trench, the smoke, the bodies, the shattered equipment. His expression was not unkind. It was worse than that. It was final. It was the look of a man who has seen the arithmetic of this place and knows the sum.

"She's a smart 'un," he said, his voice low. "Found her way before. If anyone can..." He didn't finish the sentence. The sentiment died in the foul, metallic air. *If anyone can survive this, it's not a cat. Nothing soft survives here.*

Something tightened in Tommy's chest, sharp and sudden, as if a wire had been pulled hard inside him. He swallowed and found his mouth dry. He nodded once, because that was what was expected, but his hands had begun to shake and would not stop. He kept his eyes on the ruined trench, afraid that if he looked at Mackay, or anywhere else, the thing holding him together would give way.

He had thought himself numb. He discovered, with a dull surprise, that he was not.

The day wore on, a timeless smear of fear, fatigue, and the deafening noise of nearby fighting. They repelled another probing attack. They watched, helpless, as fresh waves of their own battalion went forward from this trench towards the next German line, and were scythed down by hidden machine guns whose positions the great bombardment had miraculously missed. The "Big Push" was stalling, chewing itself to pieces in the mud, gaining yards at the cost of acres of men.

As a bruised, ugly dusk began to stain the smoke purple and grey, they were pulled back, mercifully, to consolidate and hold this captured trench for the night. They were beyond exhaustion, moving like automatons, their faces blank.

The Trench Cat of Ypres

Tommy collected his kit with numb, clumsy hands. The empty haversack felt obscenely light, a mockery. He did not look for her. Not in the shadows, not in the crannies. To look was to hope, and hope was a luxury that had died somewhere between the first whistle that morning and the first machine-gun burst that had cut down the men in the wire. Hope was for the living, and in this place, you couldn't be sure who that was.

He was sitting against the trench wall, mechanically scooping cold, congealed stew from a tin with his fingers, not tasting it, when he heard it.

Not a meow. Not a cry.

A tiny, rasping, rhythmic scrape. *Scritch. Scritch. Scritch.*

He froze, his hand halfway to his mouth. He looked around, thinking it was a rat in the walls. The sound came again. It was faint, but definite. And it came from his left, from a dark niche where a German dugout had partially collapsed, creating a shallow cave of shattered timber, torn sandbags, and pale chalk.

Slowly, like a man in a dream, he put the tin down. He crept over on hands and knees, the mud cold and slick. He peered into the darkness of the niche.

At first, nothing. Then, two pinpricks of green light reflected back at him from deep in the shadows.

And the sound again—*scritch, scritch, scritch*—urgent, focused.

Penny was there. She was deep in the shadows, her back to him. She was digging. Not a frantic, panicked scrape, but a determined, methodical excavation. Her front paws worked with a steady, alternating rhythm, pulling clumps of earth, stone, and root behind her in a growing pile.

As Tommy's eyes adjusted to the gloom, he saw why.

Curled in the hollow she was making, shielded by the curve of her own body, was a tiny, squirming, mewling knot of blind, naked life. Kittens. Three of them, their eyes sealed shut, their mouths open in silent, hungry pleas.

She must have been pregnant for weeks. In the relative safety and routine of the old front line, she had hidden it well, her thickening fur disguising her shape. The unspeakable stress and terror of the day—the bombardment, the advance, the flight into this reeking hole—had forced the birth, here, in this reeking, dark pocket of hell in the middle of Armageddon.

She paused her digging, panting lightly, her sides heaving. She turned her head and looked at him over her shoulder. Her eyes held no fear now, no panic. They held only a fierce, exhausted, primordial challenge. *This*, her gaze said, burning into his, *is my place now. These are mine. Try and move us.*

Tommy sat back on his heels, a strange, choked sound escaping him—part laugh, part sob, wholly involuntary. All around him was the grim industry of death—men a few yards away digging a makeshift grave for the day's toll, others stacking captured Mauser rifles, the distant, unending moans of the wounded in no-man's land being retrieved under the creeping dark. And here, in the midst of the unmaking, in the epicenter of the war's cruelty, was the stubborn, blind, vulnerable industry of life.

He didn't reach for her. He didn't speak. He simply nodded, once, as if accepting a report from a fellow soldier who had completed a difficult mission. Then he moved. He took his own small entrenching tool from his pack. And from the other side of the niche, careful not to crowd her, he began to carefully shore up the crumbling wall of the dugout, reinforcing it with pieces of broken timber, making the space a little safer, a little more secure against the world outside.

He worked in silence, the metal of the tool biting into the chalk with a soft *chunk*. Penny watched him for a long moment, her breathing slowing. Then she turned back to her kittens, settling her body more closely around them, tucking them in against her warmth. Her purr returned— not the steady thrum of contentment, but a ragged, weary, yet persistent sound, like a damaged engine that refuses to quit.

The Great Absence at his back was gone. It had been replaced by something infinitely heavier, and far more terrifying: a responsibility not just to keep something alive, but to help a fragile, new life *begin* in a world utterly, fanatically devoted to its destruction. He dug, and she purred, and in the gathering dark of the captured trench, the two of them worked side by side—the man and the cat—builders in the silent, determined midst of the unmakers.

Chapter 8
The Trench-Kittens

THE CAPTURED GERMAN trench, which the men had darkly christened "Kaiser's Cul-de-Sac," became a bizarre, dual-purpose world. One half remained a military position, a precarious foothold in enemy territory: sandbagged strong points at each traverse, sentries peering with red-rimmed eyes into the smoky gloom of no-man's land, the constant, whispered traffic of runners bringing orders or carrying pleas for ammunition and reinforcements back to the rear. The other half, centred on the collapsed dugout niche, was a secret, fiercely guarded nursery.

Penny was a militant, uncompromising mother. Her territory shrank to a radius of three yards from the squirming centre of her world. Woe betide any rat, mouse, or over-curious soldier who breached this invisible perimeter. A young replacement from Liverpool, drawn by the faint, high-pitched mewling like the sound of lost chicks, made the mistake of peering into the niche. He received a lightning-fast swipe that left three parallel gashes on the back of his hand, deep enough to require a field dressing and a stern talking-to from the Medical Officer about hygiene.

The lesson was learned instantly and propagated down the line with the efficiency of a military directive: *Give the cat and her brood a wide berth. No looking, no touching, no sudden movements.*

The Trench Cat of Ypres

Tommy became the sole exception. He was the quartermaster, the royal engineer, the honoured guest granted an audience. Each evening, after stand-to, he would present his tribute. It was the best of his meagre rations: the fatty, gristly bits from his Machonochie stew carefully picked out and saved; a precious sardine, pilfered from an officer's private crate at great personal risk; a small, sticky tin of condensed milk, watered down in a bottle cap and offered on the tip of a clean spoon. Penny would accept these offerings with a slow, regal blink of her bottle-green eyes. Then, as if granting a rare privilege, she would shift her body just enough to allow him a brief glimpse of the squirming, blind contents of her nest—a tangle of tiny limbs and soft, damp fur.

The kittens grew with the ruthless, accelerated speed of things that have no guarantee of a tomorrow. Their eyes opened after ten days—three pairs of hazy, milky-blue orbs peering blindly at a world of shadows, moving earth, and the giant, gentle hands of Tommy. There were two gingers, smaller, perfect replicas of their mother, and a single grey tabby with bold black stripes, who from the first was louder, more restless, more demanding than his siblings.

The men of the section, hardened by years of slaughter, their hearts calloused by loss, found themselves inexplicably, fiercely invested. The trench, a place of abstract, industrial death where men were numbers on a casualty list, now had a concrete, living, breathing project. It gave their weary minds a strange, gentle focus. They began to refer to the kittens not as a litter, but as a military unit under their collective, unofficial command.

"How's the relief company doing, Tommy?" Alfie would ask in a low voice during a lull, jerking his head towards the niche. He'd lost his earlier mocking tone; his interest was genuine, almost paternal.

"Holding the line," Tommy would reply, a ghost of a smile touching his lips. "The grey 'un's trying to mount a raid on my bootlace. Ambitious little sod."

Sergeant Mackay, on his gruff, nightly rounds to check sentries, would pause by the niche, his boots crunching on the chalky mud. He wouldn't look directly in, but would gruffly ask Tommy, "All present and correct?" And Tommy, standing a little straighter, would give a solemn report: "All present, Sarge. No casualties. Grey one's on latrine duty, keeps digging. The gingers are on watch."

It became a dark, necessary joke, a shared piece of insanity that paradoxically kept them sane. In a place where human life was cheap, snuffed out with the casual indifference of a stray shell or a sniper's bullet, these three tiny, fragile, utterly dependent lives became priceless. Their survival was a rebellion. A tiny, furry act of defiance against the universe of the trench. A statement that in this stolen patch of foreign earth, something other than death was being cultivated, nurtured, protected.

Tommy became the chief engineer of the nursery. He expanded the niche with painstaking care, using the blade of his entrenching tool like a sculptor. He shored up the walls with wood from broken ammunition boxes, weaving the slats into a lattice. He scavenged a precious, corrugated iron sheet from a shattered supply wagon and fashioned it into a sloping roof to keep out the relentless drip of rain. He lined the floor with clean straw, stolen from a derelict Belgian farmhouse behind the lines during a rare working party. It was, without a doubt, the finest, driest, most secure dugout in the entire Ypres Salient.

Penny's hunting became a strategic campaign to feed her small army. She would vanish for hours at a time, slipping into the maze of trenches and saps. She returned with grim trophies: rats, field mice, and once, triumphantly, a young, skinny rabbit she must have caught in the shell-cratered fields no-man's land had become. She was a general provisioning her troops, and the sight of her dragging a carcass twice her size down the trench became a familiar, oddly inspiring one.

The war, however, did not respect nurseries or sentiment. A week after the kittens' eyes opened, turning from milky blue to the green of their mother, the Germans zeroed in on their section of the captured trench with a mortar barrage. It was sudden, a shrieking rain of iron that gave no time for anything but instinct. *Whoomp. Whoosh. CRUMP.* Dirt and smoke and deadly fragments filled the air.

Tommy, caught on the firestep trying to spot a sniper, threw himself into a traverse, pressing his face into the cold mud as the world exploded around him. The concussions punched the air from his lungs. When the barrage lifted as abruptly as it began, and the ringing in his ears subsided to a high whine, his first thought was not for Alfie, nor for the Sergeant. It was a bolt of pure, undiluted ice to his heart. He scrambled, half-crawling, through the freshly churned earth and debris, towards the niche.

The corrugated iron roof was dented and scarred, covered in a layer of dirt and stone chips, but it had held. With trembling hands, he pulled it aside.

Inside, in the dim light, Penny was spread over her kittens like a living, breathing blanket. Her body was rigid, every muscle taut. Her ears were flat against her skull. She was panting, her tongue slightly out, and a trickle of blood matted the fur on her shoulder—a flying splinter of stone or shrapnel. Beneath her, sheltered by the arch of her body and the curve of the nest, the three kittens mewled in frightened protest, but they were whole. Unharmed.

Her eyes met his. They were wide, but not with the blind fear of the bombardment. They blazed with a feral, defensive fury. She had felt the world try to kill her children, had heard the shriek of the shells meant for them, and she had stood her ground. She had absorbed the terror and held the line.

"Alright, girl," Tommy breathed, his own hands shaking so badly he could barely wipe the dirt from his face. "Alright. You held the line. Good girl."

He cleaned her wound as best he could with a corner of his handkerchief and a little water from his bottle. It was a shallow graze, already clotting. She endured his ministrations with a stiff, silent dignity, never taking her eyes off the trench beyond the niche, as if expecting another assault at any moment. From that day, she rarely left the kittens. Her trust in Tommy's provisions became absolute; her hunting forays ceased. The defence of the nursery was now her sole, all-consuming purpose.

The kittens, oblivious to their brush with annihilation, began to explore. Their world was the small, safe universe of the straw-lined niche and the immediate vicinity of Tommy's legs when he sat with them. The two gingers were cautious, peering out from the safety of the entrance with wide, wondering eyes before retreating to the familiar warmth of their mother's flank. The grey tabby, whom Alfie had christened "The Major" for his bossy, commanding mewls, was the explorer, the platoon's point man.

He would bat with deadly seriousness at loose threads on Tommy's puttees, attempt to scale the sandbag wall of the trench (and tumble back down in a soft, surprised heap), and once, to uproarious laughter from the men watching, plunged comically into a half-full mess tin of cold stew, emerging sputtering and indignant.

His first true foray beyond the safe zone happened on a rare, quiet afternoon. Tommy was sitting on an ammo box, sewing a button back onto his tunic. The Major, stalking a bit of drifting thistledown carried on the breeze, followed his prey with single-minded determination around the corner of the traverse and out of sight.

A minute later, a roar of laughter—real laughter, not the grim bark of the trenches—echoed down the communication trench. Tommy jumped up, heart in his throat. Rounding the corner, he found a circle of grimy soldiers from the next platoon, their rifles leaning against the wall, grins splitting their dirty faces. In the centre of the circle, sitting atop a large coil of signal wire as if it were a throne, was The Major. He was washing a paw with an air of utter, regal unconcern, as if presiding over a court of particularly grubby subjects.

"Says 'ere he's inspectin' the communications, Sarge," one of the men, a wiry Scot, joked to his nonplussed sergeant. "Found a weak spot in the wire and everything. Reckon he wants a promotion."

The grey kitten was returned with much ceremony, handed over to Tommy like a visiting dignitary, along with a tribute of a small, precious piece of fried bacon. The incident broke the final, unofficial barrier. The trench-kittens were no longer Tommy and Penny's secret; they were the platoon's mascots, the company's dirty little secret. Their survival became a point of collective, fierce pride. They were a tiny, vulnerable flame of normalcy, of life, and every man in that stretch of trench felt sworn by an unspoken oath to protect it.

One evening, as Tommy fed Penny her condensed milk,

Lieutenant Chambers appeared. He looked more hollowed out than ever, a boy playing dress-up in a man's nightmare, but his eyes held a soft, wondering light as he looked past Tommy into the niche, at the cat and the three little heads now poking out curiously from behind her.

"Remarkable," he murmured, not to Tommy, but to the universe. "In this place... of all places... they are quite remarkable." He didn't stay long, embarrassed perhaps by his own sentiment. But later, a runner arrived with a small, heavy tin. "For the relief company, from HQ," the boy said with a wink. The tin was high-grade tuna, clearly from an officer's private stock, a treasure beyond measure.

The kittens opened their eyes wider, learned to pounce on shadows and skittering beetles, and filled the foul trench air with their tiny, ridiculous squeaks and mock-ferocious growls. They were a living paradox: the most vulnerable things in a world of steel and high explosives, and yet, in their complete dependence and their stubborn, burgeoning vitality, they became the strongest thing in it. They were the secret, beating heart of Kaiser's Cul-de-Sac, a tiny, furry pulse that reminded every man who saw them of what they were, in their deepest souls, fighting for—not for king, nor country, nor glory, nor even for the man next to them, but for the simple, sacred, defiant right of life to continue. To grow. To purr in a pile of stolen straw, in the face of the gathering dark.

The war outside the niche raged on, a distant thunder. But inside, behind the lattice of ammo-box wood and the dented iron roof, a different kind of campaign was being waged, and won. One small, blind, purring victory at a time.

Chapter 9
The Silent Offensive

THE STALEMATE SOLIDIFIED like the trench mud in a new frost. The "Big Push" had bled itself out against the German machine guns, gaining a few hundred yards of useless, crater-pocked earth at a cost no sergeant major's clipboard could tally. Their battalion was pulled back, not to the promised "rest" billets with estaminets and real beds, but to a different, quieter sector of the line—a stretch of low, waterlogged ground near Boesinghe where the water table was higher than the trench bottoms. Here, the trenches were more like canals, and the primary enemy was less the German infantry across the way than the creeping, insidious damp that rotted everything it touched.

Their new home was a place of perpetual ooze. The walls wept continuously, a cold sweat of condensation. Duckboards floated on a soup of mud, and walking the line meant balancing like a tightrope walker over a foul-smelling abyss. Rats swam rather than scurried. It was a battle against trench foot that turned feet to black, necrotic pulp, against pneumonia that rattled in lungs already weakened by gas, and against a soul-crushing, grey misery that seeped in deeper than the water.

The move was a perilous exodus for the nursery. Tommy, with Sergeant Mackay's gruff, tacit approval, was given a sandbag as transport. He lined it with the last of the clean straw, placed Penny and the three squirming, half-grown kittens inside, and carried the bag through the labyrinth of communication trenches like a holy relic, a strange, living parcel.

Penny, for once, did not protest or try to escape. She kept her head poked out of the bag's opening, her eyes scanning the new, dripping, dismal world with a profound, whisker-twitching suspicion.

The kittens, now five weeks old and bundles of chaotic, oversized-pawed energy, tumbled over each other inside the dark sack, treating the lurching journey as a grand, mysterious adventure, their tiny mews of protest sounding from within.

Their new dugout was a dank, low-ceilinged cave that smelled of wet dog, decay, and the sharp, fungal scent of white rot eating the timber props. Water pooled in the corners. Tommy set to work immediately, driven by a need to provide stability. He built a raised platform from more scavenged ammunition boxes, creating a dry island in the centre of the muddy floor.

Penny approved of the platform with a slow blink. She disapproved of everything else. The rats here were different—lean, aquatic, and bold, with a greasy look to their fur. The familiar hunting grounds and hidden runs of the old trench were gone. The sounds were wrong: fewer of the deep-throated roars of heavy artillery, more of the sniper's solitary, spiteful *crack* that came without warning, and the endless, maddening *drip-drip-drip* from the ceiling, a Chinese water torture of the senses.

The kittens, however, thrived on the new textures. The two gingers, whom Tommy had named *Rust* (for his quiet, reddish coat) and *Ginger* (for her brighter, fiercer hue), were mesmerised by the reflections in the standing water, batting at phantom fish with soft, serious paws. *The Major*, the grey tabby, launched a fearless and wildly unsuccessful offensive against the persistent drip from a leak in the roof, leaping again and again to bat at the falling water until he was soaked, sputtering, and supremely indignant, much to the men's amusement.

But a new, silent enemy was on the march, one that no raised platform could defend against.

It began with a cough. Not the dry, dusty rasp of a gas victim, or the tubercular rattle of an old miner, but a deep, wet, wrenching cough that seemed to come from the very boots of Private Davies, the young replacement. It sounded like something tearing loose inside his chest. Within two days, he was burning with fever, his skin slick with sweat despite the chill damp of the dugout. His eyes glittered with unnatural brightness. He was carried away on a stretcher, his face the colour of slate, his breath a horrible, bubbling gurgle.

Then Alfie started. A tickle in the throat at first, which he dismissed with a joke about "Flanders' finest air." Then the full, body-shaking spasm that doubled him over, leaving him gasping. Then Perkins, the boy who had found solace in Penny's purr. It moved through the trench with the speed and ruthlessness of a machine-gun burst along a parapet. The Spanish Flu, they called it, though it had nothing to do with Spain. It was a ghost sickness, carried on the damp, crowded air, killing more efficiently and impersonally than any artillery barrage. It didn't discriminate between brave and coward, veteran and greenhorn. It simply harvested.

The trench became a charnel house in slow motion. Healthy men moved like ghosts themselves, their faces masks of dread beneath their respirators (worn now against contagion, not gas), tending to the sick. The coughing was a constant, day-and-night chorus, undercut with moans and the horrible, liquid struggle for air that ended in silence. Bodies were removed with a grim, quiet regularity before first light, wrapped in groundsheets, their identities sometimes forgotten in the feverish haste.

Penny sensed it immediately. This enemy had no sound of approach, no smell of cordite or chlorine. It was a silent, creeping poison in the air itself. She gathered her kittens onto the highest, driest part of the platform and refused to let them down. Her hunting ceased entirely. She lived solely on the scraps Tommy could bring, her eyes fixed on her charges with a vigilance that bordered on quiet mania. She would hiss, low and warning, at any man who came too close coughing.

Tommy felt the first tickle in his own throat three days after Alfie was carried out, delirious, calling for his mother. A cold dread, colder than the trench water, seeped into him. It was a different fear than that of shells —this was an internal enemy, a betrayal by one's own body. He doubled his efforts, using his last precious bar of chocolate to bribe a cook for extra scraps of meat for Penny, smuggling an extra blanket to line their platform, knowing what might be coming. He watched The Major pounce on a water-skater skating on a puddle and felt a pang of such acute love and terror it stole his breath—or perhaps that was the fever, beginning its work.

When the fever hit, it hit like a shell-blast to the senses. One moment he was shivering uncontrollably by the brazier, the next he was on the platform, though he had no memory of climbing onto it. He was burning and freezing all at once, his muscles screaming as if he'd been on a forced march for days. The world swam in and out of focus, the dugout walls melting and reforming into the streets of Durham. He heard Mackay's voice, sounding very far away: "Finch is down. Get the orderlies."

He was aware of being moved, of rough hands under

his armpits, his feet dragging in the mud. He tried to protest, to croak something about the cats, about the platform, but only a wet, incoherent rasp came out. Then he was in the medical dugout, a fetid, overcrowded pit of misery stacked with sick men on stretchers laid directly on the mud. The air was thick and hot with the smell of vomit, sweat, carbolic, and death. The world narrowed to the fiery agony in his chest, the taste of blood in his mouth, and the blurred, suffering faces of strangers around him.

Time lost all meaning. He drifted in a haze of delirium. He dreamed of flowers moving in the grasses of the Durham moors, of the sun on the slag heaps, of his mother's kitchen smelling of baking bread; of Penny sitting regally on a sandbag in a clean, dry trench; and of the kittens tumbling into a bottomless, watery crater that was also his own lungs.

He woke to a cool hand on his brow. He forced his eyes open. A medical orderly he did not recognize was looking down at him, his face exhausted but his eyes holding a faint, professional spark. "You're a lucky one, mate. Fever broke in the night. You'll live. Weak as a kitten, but you'll live."

Tommy tried to speak. His throat was raw fire. "The... cat," he managed, the words tearing. "My dugout... platform..."

The orderly frowned, wiping his brow with a damp cloth. "What? Don't worry about your kit, son. Just rest."

But the thought of them—alone, with him gone, with the sickness thick in the air of their dugout—was a hook in his mind, pulling him back towards consciousness. Using strength he didn't know he had, he pushed himself up on his elbows. The world swayed nauseatingly. In the cot next to him, a shape lay still under a blanket, the face covered. It was Alfie's build. The hook pulled harder, deep into his gut.

He waited until the orderly was bent over another man, listening to his chest. Then, moving like an old man, he swung his leaden legs off the cot. The floor was icy mud. He stood, swaying, clutching a timber prop for support. He was clad only in his filthy underclothes, trembling with weakness. He didn't care. He staggered towards the dugout entrance, past rows of sick and dying men who didn't give him a second glance, their worlds shrunk to their own private hells.

The trench outside was a grey, dripping nightmare in the flat light of late afternoon. He didn't know how long he'd been gone. A day? Three? The flu warped time. He stumbled, fell to his knees in the mud, crawled a few yards, then hauled himself up again, driven by the single, pulsing thought. *The platform. The ammunition box platform. The nest.*

He reached his section's stretch of trench. It was eerily quiet. Many of the familiar faces were absent. He saw Sergeant Mackay coming out of a dugout, his face grim. Mackay saw him and stopped dead, his eyes widening as if seeing a ghost. He opened his mouth, but Tommy shook his head, a tiny, desperate movement, and kept staggering forward. Mackay didn't stop him.

Tommy half-fell, half-crawled into the entrance of his own dugout. The smell was different—not just damp and decay, but a clean, sharp, musky scent of... life. Of animal.

On the raised platform, in a nest of torn blanket and the last of the straw, lay Penny. She was thinner, her luxurious winter coat now dull and patchy. But her eyes were bright and alert, burning in her gaunt face. And curled against her, sleeping in a purring, tangled pile of limbs and tails, were three gangly, half-grown kittens.

The Trench Cat of Ypres

Rust, Ginger, and The Major. They had grown in his absence. Beside her front paws, laid neatly like a gruesome offering, was a freshly killed, large rat.

She looked at him as he crawled in, filthy, shaking, and spectral. She didn't get up. She didn't meow. She just gave a slow, deliberate blink, then lowered her head to gently nuzzle The Major's ear. *We held the line*, her entire exhausted posture said. *We waited. We survived. We hunted.*

Tommy collapsed onto the muddy floor beside the platform, his fever-weakened body giving out completely. He didn't have the strength to climb up. He simply lay there, his cheek against the cold, rough wood of the ammunition box, his hand reaching up, fingers trembling.

Penny, after a moment's quiet consideration, stretched her neck down from the platform. She butted her head against his trembling fingers. Then a rough, sandpaper tongue licked his knuckle, once, twice.

From above, the silent, invisible offensive of the Spanish Flu had swept through the trench like a scythe, taking Alfie, taking Perkins, taking so many. It had lapped at the edges of the platform, the air thick with its poison. But it had not taken this. In this damp, dark, dying hole, a cat had kept the flame of her tiny, ridiculous, magnificent family alive. She had hunted when she was starving, had warmed them when the deadly chill seeped in, and had stood a silent, stubborn vigil over life itself against a ghost.

As the tremors of fever and exhaustion finally subsided, replaced by a deep, bone-marrow weariness, Tommy listened. Under the distant drip from the ceiling, under the far-off, wracking cough from another dugout, was a softer, layered sound. The ragged, weary rumble of Penny's purr, and the higher, lighter, contented purrs of the three kittens, all tangled together in sleep.

It was the sound of a victory. Not a martial victory with flags and captured guns. A small, silent, furry victory. Won not with a charge over the top, but with a mother's stubborn, unblinking vigil in the dark.

Chapter 10
The Breaking Point

THE FLU RECEDED like a foul tide, leaving the trench depleted, hollowed-out, and numb. The silence it left behind was different from the quiet after a barrage. That was a ringing, shocked silence. This was a silence of absence, of missing voices, of gaps on the firestep where a man should be standing. It was a quieter, more profound subtraction. Alfie was gone. Perkins was gone. Johnson, the former butcher, was gone. Nearly a third of the section, erased not by steel, but by a ghost in the lungs.

Sergeant Mackay moved through the days like a man carved from the same grey, waterlogged timber that propped up the trench walls. His voice, once a gravelly instrument of command, had subsided to a flat, toneless monotone. Lieutenant Chambers was transferred out, rumoured to be suffering from "neurasthenia"—a polite, clinical word for a mind shattered by the relentless calculus of loss. New replacements arrived, boys with unscarred faces and kit that still smelled of warehouse storage. They flinched at the sound of a sniper's rifle with a fresh, undulled terror, and stared with morbid, wide-eyed fascination at the waterlogged, corpse-strewn expanse of no-man's land. The veterans, the few who were left, didn't bother learning their names. What was the point?

In the midst of this grey, soul-numbing aftermath, the kittens became the trench's nervous system, its only source of undiluted, vibrant life. They were no longer tiny balls of fluff but lanky, oversized-pawed adolescents, their personalities solidifying into distinct roles within their furry platoon.

Rust, the male ginger, was the scout. Quiet, cautious, and possessed of an uncanny, silent cleverness. He had mastered the art of moving through the trench unseen—a shadow along the parapet, a flicker in a traverse. He was the first to detect the distant rumble of an approaching ration party, the first to notice a new face in a neighboring bay. He brought intelligence back to the platform not in reports, but in the form of dropped haversack straps, discarded cigarette packets, or a particular, intent way of staring down a communication trench.

Ginger, his sister, was the combat engineer. She was fascinated by structure, by how things were made and held together. She would spend hours patting at the weave of a sandbag, testing the stability of a stacked crate with a careful paw, batting at the persistent drips from the roof with a focused, problem-solving intensity. On one memorable occasion, she had managed to worry loose a timber that was threatening to collapse part of their platform, earning a rare, approving head-butt from Penny —the feline equivalent of a medal.

The Major was, as ever, the infantry. Bold to the point of glorious, reckless stupidity, he regarded the entire captured trench as his personal empire to be pacified and conquered. He led frontal assaults on rats twice his size, got his head stuck in empty bully beef tins requiring rescue, and once, to Tommy's heart-stopping horror, sauntered out onto a quiet stretch of no-man's land at dawn to chase a drifting feather. It necessitated a frantic, low-crawl rescue mission under the watchful eye of a German sniper who, miraculously, held his fire—whether

The Trench Cat of Ypres

out of amusement, shared humanity, or sheer disbelief, Tommy never knew.

Their existence was the one flicker of colour, of uncomplicated purpose, in Tommy's grey world. Cleaning his rifle, he'd have Ginger inspecting the moving bolt with academic interest. Trying to write a letter home (increasingly impossible, as the words seemed to have dried up and blown away), The Major would attack the moving pencil, a fearsome hunter of graphite. On the long, cold hours of sentry duty, Rust would materialise silently beside him, a small, warm presence sharing the watch on the dark, his quiet company a comfort.

But the war was grinding down, and not just the men. The news from home, when it came, was of strikes and shortages, of a war-weariness that mirrored their own. The news from the front was of more failed, limited offensives, more names on lengthening memorial lists. A deep, cynical rot set in among the survivors. They weren't fighting for king and country anymore—those were abstractions that had died in the mud of Passchendaele. They weren't even fighting for the man next to them; too many of those men were gone. They were just trying to survive the next hour, the next day, until their number came up in the great, indifferent lottery. They were marking time in a condemned cell.

The breaking point came not with a bang, or a gas attack, or a raid. It came on a dry, windy afternoon with a piece of paper and a man with polished boots.

A new commander, a Colonel from Division HQ, came on an inspection tour. He was brisk, red-tabbed, with a neatly trimmed moustache and eyes like chips of grey flint that missed nothing and forgave less. He strode down the trench, his polished boots skimming the duckboards with a disdainful precision, his nose wrinkled at the compounded smells of mud, men, and decay. His aide, a pale lieutenant, trailed behind him, clipboard at the ready.

The Colonel's flinty eyes took in everything: the weeping walls, the weary, unshaven men who saluted with a lethargy bordering on insolence, the general air of sullen endurance. And then they landed on the carefully shored-up platform in Tommy's dugout alcove.

On that platform, The Major was in the midst of a spirited, rolling wrestling match with a piece of dirty bandage. Ginger was observing from a crate, her tail twitching with tactical interest. Rust was washing his paws with fastidious care. Penny observed them all from a higher perch on a stack of ration tins, the picture of maternal tolerance, her chin resting on her paws.

The Colonel stopped dead. His aide almost walked into him.

"What," the Colonel said, his voice cutting through the low trench murmur like a wire-cutter through flesh, "is *that?*"

Sergeant Mackay stepped forward, saluting. "Mascots, sir. Trench cats. Been with the section for months. Excellent for morale, sir. And rodent control." He said it flatly, a statement of fact.

The Colonel's face did not change. It remained a mask of polished disapproval. "Rodent control." He made it sound like a feeble, pathetic excuse. His gaze swept over the four felines with the cold assessment of a man inspecting faulty equipment. "This is a forward combat position, Sergeant. Not a petting zoo. It is unsanitary."

He paused, letting the word hang. "It is undisciplined."

He turned to his aide. "Note this location. Have the Royal Army Veterinary Corps detachment remove these animals at the earliest opportunity. They are to be taken to the rear and..." He paused again, finding the right, bureaucratic word. "...*disposed of.*"

The word dropped into the damp, still air of the trench like a lead weight. *Disposed of.* Like broken rifles. Like spoiled rations. Like waste.

Tommy felt the world tilt on its axis. He wasn't aware of moving, but he found himself standing before the Colonel, his hands clenched into white-knuckled fists at his sides, his heart hammering against his ribs like a bird in a cage.

"Sir," he said, his voice strange and thin to his own ears.

The Colonel looked at him as if he were a curious, slightly offensive insect that had crawled onto his map. "Yes, Private?"

"They're not... they're not just animals, sir." The words felt stupid, inadequate. "They're... they've been here. Through everything. They're part of the section."

"They are a hygiene hazard and a distraction from duty," the Colonel finished, his tone final, bored. He glanced at the platform with distaste, as if it were a pile of rubbish. "Sentimentality has no place here, Private. This is a war. Not a children's story."

He looked past Tommy to Mackay. "See it's done, Sergeant." And with that, he moved on, his aide scurrying to catch up, leaving a frozen, silent wake behind him.

The trench seemed to stop breathing. The men looked from Tommy's pale, stricken face to the cats, who were blissfully unaware that their world had just been condemned by a man in clean boots. Penny, sensitive to the violent shift in the emotional weather, jumped down from her perch and stood beside Tommy, her tail twitching in a low, anxious rhythm.

Sergeant Mackay approached slowly. His face was

grim, etched with lines of weary resignation. "Orders are orders, Finch." He said it quietly.

"They'll kill them, Sarge," Tommy whispered, the horror of it washing over him in a cold, sick wave. After the shells, the gas, the flu... to be taken by their own side. To be led away and "disposed of." It was the ultimate, senseless betrayal.

"I know," Mackay said, his voice so low only Tommy could hear. Then he did something extraordinary. He looked Tommy directly in the eye, and in that look was a lifetime of understanding, of shared misery, of battles fought and men lost.

"The RAVC lads," he murmured, "they're based back at Brigade. Won't be able to come up for details like this before dusk. Lot of paperwork to process, see." He held Tommy's gaze for a long, significant second. "Lot can happen before dusk."

He turned away abruptly, his voice rising to its usual gravelly command. "Davies! Get that firing step repaired! Look lively!"

The message was as clear as a written order, and infinitely more fragile. *You have until dusk.*

Tommy looked at the platform, at his family. He had led them into this. He had bought Penny for a shilling. He had brought her to this trench in his haversack. He had helped her build her nursery in a shell-hole under fire. He had fed them, protected them, loved them. And now, because of a man offended by their existence, he had to save them. Or try.

He couldn't fight the Colonel. He couldn't fight the whole British Army and its love of tidiness. But he could fight for this one, tiny, furry square yard of defiance. He could try.

He knelt down on the muddy duckboards. Penny came

to him immediately, rubbing her flank against his leg, a soft question in her eyes. The Major abandoned his bandage and pounced on his boot. Ginger and Rust watched, curious.

"Right," Tommy said, his voice thick with an emotion he couldn't name. "New orders. We're going on a patrol. A long one."

The plan formed in the white-hot forge of his desperation. He would take them out. Not back through the communication trenches—they'd be seen, stopped. Out. Over the top. Into the blasted wilderness of no-man's land, and through it. To the fields and shattered woods behind what were n*ow* the German lines, but had been Belgian farmland. Maybe, just maybe, there was a barn, a cellar, a forgotten place beyond the reach of red-tabbed colonels and disposal orders. A ditch that wasn't owned by any army.

It was madness. It was suicide. It was the only card he had left to play, and it was a deuce.

As the grey afternoon light began to fade to a deeper, more forgiving gloom, Tommy prepared. He emptied his haversack of everything non-essential—spare socks, his mess tin, his paybook. He kept only his water bottle, his revolver (with six precious rounds), and a small, hard packet of emergency ration chocolate. He lined the bottom with his last clean shirt, a soft, worn cotton that smelled of home.

He looked at the four of them, gathered now, sensing his tension.

"Come on then," he said, his heart a cold, hard stone of dread in his chest.

One by one, they came. Rust first, slinking into the open bag with a quiet understanding, as if this were just another reconnaissance. Then Ginger, after a moment's thoughtful pause, assessing the space before stepping delicately inside. The Major needed to be corralled, but went in with a final, playful swat at Tommy's fingers. Last was Penny.

She stood before the open bag, looking up at Tommy, then back at the dugout alcove—her kingdom through winter, gas, flu, and bombardment. The platform he'd built. The straw nest. She gave a soft, sighing *mrrp*, a sound of profound farewell. Then she walked forward, stepped delicately over the edge, and curled herself around her children, a living blanket.

Tommy fastened the flap, leaving it open a crack for air. He shouldered the bag. It was heavier than it had ever been—the weight of four lives, of a decision, of a terrible, loving gamble. He slung his rifle over his other shoulder.

At the entrance to the dugout, he paused and looked back at the empty platform, the silent, waiting trench. Sergeant Mackay was at the far end, his back turned, studying a map with fierce, pretended concentration. He didn't look up.

Tommy turned. He took a deep, shuddering breath of the damp, foul, familiar air. Then he began to climb the muddy, makeshift ladder to the firestep. The setting sun was a blood-orange smear on the western horizon, painting the sea of craters in long, grasping shadows. Somewhere down the line, a lone machine gun tapped out a bored, sporadic rhythm, as if counting down the seconds.

He adjusted the weight on his back, feeling the living warmth and slight, restless movement through the canvas. The bag shifted as The Major repositioned himself.

"Alright," Tommy whispered, to them, to himself, to the uncaring, darkening sky. "Let's go find a better ditch."

The Trench Cat of Ypres

And with that, he hoisted himself over the sandbagged parapet, out of the trench, and into the open, waiting mouth of no-man's land.

Chapter 11
No-Man's Land

THE WORLD BEYOND the parapet was a different planet, a landscape born from a nightmare. The trench, for all its horrors, had been a lane, a channel, a defined space with walls and a sense, however false, of order. This was formless, endless, a shattered geometry under a vast, indifferent sky bruised purple and grey by the dying sun. Craters overlapped like the cells of a rotten honeycomb, some filled with oily, reflective water that gleamed with a sickly sheen, others dark with shadows so deep they seemed to swallow light. The smell was overwhelming—a layered assault of wet earth, old cordite, the sharp, metallic scent of rusting metal, and the high, sweet, cloying reek of decay that no wind, however constant, could ever disperse.

Tommy moved in a low, scrambling crouch, his body bent double, his eyes scanning the gloom for any movement, any shape that wasn't earth. Every shadow in a crater lip was a potential sniper. Every dark lump in the mud was a corpse, or a piece of one. The haversack bounced against his back with each cautious step, and he heard a muffled, questioning *mrrp* from within.

"Quiet now," he breathed, not sure if he was talking to the cats or to the frantic hammering of his own heart. "Just... be quiet."

He navigated by memory and a desperate, internal compass, aiming for a distant, shattered copse of trees

The Trench Cat of Ypres

that marked the old German front line, now just a ruin. It was maybe two hundred yards away. In training, he could cover that in under thirty seconds. Here, it might as well have been two hundred miles. The ground was a treacherous soup of mud, hidden shell fragments, tangles of rusted wire that snagged at his puttees, and unseen holes that threatened to twist an ankle with every step.

He froze as a flare burst overhead with a soft *pop,* then a hiss. It was German, a magnesium-white star that drifted down on its little parachute, casting long, dancing, grotesque shadows that made the craters seem to writhe and breathe. He dropped into the nearest shell hole, pressing himself into the cold mud, the haversack a conspicuous, living lump on his back. The light bleached all colour from the world, exposing every terrible detail in stark, shadowless clarity: the shreds of a grey uniform on a skeletal bush, the glint of a broken bottle that had once held schnapps, the wide, surprised eyes of a man curled peacefully as if sleeping, half-submerged in the crater's oily water.

In the stark, unforgiving light, something moved. A rat, sleek and obscenely fat, nosed at the dead man's outstretched hand. Then another emerged from a hole in the crater wall. A whole pack of them, moving with a bold, proprietorial air under the illuminating flare, masters of this domain.

The haversack on his back jerked violently. A low, primal growl vibrated through the canvas, so deep and fierce Tommy felt it in his spine. It was Penny's voice, but transformed—a sound of pure, territorial fury that cut through her fear. *This is my prey. This is my world.* The rats scattered, vanishing into their holes as if commanded, just as the flare sputtered and died, plunging the land back into murky, merciful twilight.

Silence rushed back in, thicker and more profound than before. Tommy waited, ears straining, tasting mud and his own fear. No shout of alarm from the German lines, no rifle shot. The rats had been the only witnesses to his passage.

He crawled out of the crater and moved on, his journey a nightmarish pilgrimage through a garden of the dead. He passed a British Mark IV tank, "Crustacean" painted in fading, ironic letters on its side, its nose buried in a crater, its sponsors like broken, metallic wings. He skirted a field of barbed wire so thick and tangled it looked like a black, thorny fungus growing from the very earth. He stepped over things—a boot with a foot still in it, the scattered pages of a German Bible, a harmonica—refusing to let his eyes focus, to let them become real.

The kittens were silent now. He could feel their tense, absolute stillness through the canvas. They were hunters born in a trench, but this was the source, the vast, open charnel house from which all their smaller prey ultimately came. This was the truth their mother had always smelled on the wind, the reality she had warned them about from the firestep.

He reached the shattered trees, what was left of the old German front line. The trench here was a shallow, collapsed ditch, full of broken equipment, empty ammunition boxes, and more of the dead. He couldn't stay. He had to keep going, through what had been their support lines, into the land beyond, the shattered hinterland.

As he prepared to move from the cover of the trench ruin, a new sound froze him solid. Not guns. Not shells.

Voices. German voices, low and conversational, coming from a reinforced bunker entrance just twenty yards to his left, partially caved in but clearly still occupied. A sentry post, or a sheltered spot for a machine-gun team taking a break.

He pressed himself against the chalky back of the captured trench, barely breathing. The haversack was an impossible burden of potential sound and movement. He willed the cats to stillness, to the understanding they had shown in the sap.

One of the Germans laughed, a young, tired sound. A match flared, illuminating for a second two pale, young faces under the distinctive rim of their coal-scuttle helmets as they lit cigarettes. They were looking out across their own stretch of no-man's land, away from him, their backs partially turned. But if one of them turned to toss the match…

A tiny, almost inaudible squeak came from the bag. A kitten's squeak of protest against prolonged confinement and jostling. The Major, stating his displeasure.

One of the Germans paused, his cigarette halfway to his lips. He said something to his comrade, who shrugged and murmured a reply. They were listening, their heads cocked.

Tommy's hand found the cool, checkered grip of his Webley revolver. It was a useless, suicidal gesture. Firing would bring the whole trench down on him. His mind raced, blank with terror.

Then, from the darkness near the Germans' feet, came a dry scuttle. A large rat, emboldened by the quiet and the scent of food, darted across the broken ground in front of their position. The German who had paused chuckled, said something clearly meaning "just a rat," and took a deep, relaxing drag of his cigarette. The moment of tension passed. They turned back to their watch, to their smoke, to the vast, stupid boredom of war.

Tommy didn't wait. As they gazed outwards, he

slithered like a snake over the far side of the trench ruin and into the deeper, more open darkness beyond, moving now not towards any specific safety, but simply *away* from the lines, from the war, from the Colonel's order.

He walked for an hour, or maybe two. Time had lost all meaning, stretched and compressed by fear. The landscape began to change, subtly. The sheer, concentrated density of destruction lessened. There were still craters, still the scattered detritus of battle, but there were also stretches of torn, muddy grass struggling through the churned earth, the black skeleton of a farmhouse against the sky, the vague outlines of what had once been a field, its furrows still visible under the scars.

Exhaustion, deeper and more total than any he'd known in the trench or on a route march, dragged at him. His legs were leaden pillars. The haversack straps cut into his shoulders like wire. His mouth was dust-dry. He found a shell hole far from any visible trench line, deep and relatively dry, with an overhang of earth and root that offered a semblance of cover from the sky and from casual view. It would have to do. He could go no further.

He carefully lowered the bag onto the dryish earth and opened the flap.

Four faces peered out, eyes huge and luminous in the dark. One by one, they emerged, blinking, into the vast, open world. Rust first, sniffing the air with academic caution, his whiskers forward. Then Ginger, who immediately began a meticulous inspection of the crumbly soil of the hole's wall, as if assessing its defensive potential. The Major tumbled out with a small, indignant meow, shook himself vigorously from nose to tail-tip, and then sat down hard, overwhelmed. Lastly, Penny stepped out with her usual quiet dignity. She ignored the surroundings for a moment, turning instead to

The Trench Cat of Ypres

thoroughly wash The Major's face with her rough tongue, tidying him up after the unscheduled journey, restoring order.

Tommy slumped against the earth wall of the crater, watching them. In this vast, silent grave under the stars, they were performing the ancient, comforting rituals of home. Ginger found a beetle and batted it with thoughtful curiosity. Rust sat quietly by Tommy's side, a small, warm sentinel. Penny finished her grooming, gave herself a brisk shake, and then, sitting neatly, began to purr. It was a steady, calm, rhythmic thrum in the immense quiet of the night, a sound utterly defiant of the desolation around them.

He pulled out the water bottle and the hard slab of ration chocolate. He broke the chocolate into pieces, placing them on a relatively clean stone. The kittens fell upon the unfamiliar treat with enthusiasm. Penny ate hers slowly, with delicate bites, then came over and head-butted his hand. He poured a little water into his cupped palm and she lapped at it, her rough tongue tickling his skin, her purr never ceasing.

Overhead, for the first time in years, he really saw the stars. They were shockingly bright, unpolluted by the fire-trench's constant glow or the smoke of battle. A universe of cold, distant fire. Somewhere, far away from this crater, a nightingale sang, its melody heartbreakingly beautiful and utterly, surrealistically incongruous. For a moment, the war was just a rumour, a bad dream lingering on the edges of this quiet, cratered field. The front was a distant murmur to the west. The Colonel's order was just words on paper, lost in some headquarters far behind.

The Major, his hunger satisfied and his face cleaned, climbed into Tommy's lap. He turned three times, kneaded Tommy's muddy trousers with his paws, then curled into a tight circle and began to knead and purr, a tiny, vibrating engine of contentment. Rust settled against his leg. Ginger finished her geological survey and sat, wrapping her tail neatly around her feet. Penny leaned her warm, solid weight against his side.

Tommy sat in the shell hole, a man in a hole in the middle of a continent being torn apart, surrounded by cats. He was a deserter. He was beyond the lines, in a terrifying no-place. He was utterly, completely lost, with no plan beyond the next sunrise.

And yet, as The Major's purr vibrated through his thighs and Penny's warmth seeped into his side, he felt a peace so profound it brought a hot, stinging pressure behind his eyes. The grinding fear of the trench, the weight of orders, the stench of death, the blind, animal terror of the barrage—it was all behind him. The responsibility on his shoulders was immense, terrifying—to keep these four lives alive in this wilderness—but it was clean. It was not to kill, or to hold a piece of meaningless, bloody ground. It was simply to protect. To find them a morning that wasn't heralded by a bombardment, a patch of earth that wasn't owned by any army.

He put a hand on Penny's back, feeling the powerful purr resonate up his arm, into his bones. He looked up at the cold, indifferent, beautiful stars.

"Right," he whispered into the fur and the vast, listening dark. "First light, we find a barn."

It was a promise. A prayer. The first step in a plan that had no second step, in a future that stretched no further than the next ridge. But for now, in the crater, with the purring, it was enough.

His eyes grew heavy. The exhaustion of the day, the night, the years, pressed down on him. The warmth of the cats, the profound silence, the sheer impossibility of where he was... it all blurred into a soft, welcoming haze.

He drifted, not into sleep, but into a dream that felt more real than the mud beneath him. A dream of a sunlit barn, of kittens tumbling in hay, of a world without the sound of guns...

Chapter 12
The Reckoning

THE FANTASY OF the crater shattered like glass under a boot.

A hand clamped on Tommy's shoulder, shaking him roughly. "Finch. *Finch!*"

The voice was a low, urgent growl. The dream of hay and sunlight and silent stars dissolved into the familiar, hated outline of a corrugated iron roof, stained with mildew and candle soot. The smell was not clean night air, but the close, fetid stink of the dugout—damp wool, stale tobacco, unwashed men, and the sweet, decaying undertone of the trench itself.

He was not in a crater. He was on the raised platform in Kaiser's Cul-de-Sac. Penny was curled against his side, but her body was rigid, her ears flat against her skull. The kittens were a silent, watchful pile in the straw, their eyes gleaming in the gloom.

One of the newer recruit's faces loomed over him, hollow-eyed and unshaven in the guttering light of a single candle. A fresh crack ran through one of his front teeth, a souvenir of a recent ration-box struggle. "You were muttering in your sleep," he whispered, his voice raspy, his eyes darting towards the dugout entrance. "Something about a barn. For Christ's sake, man, keep it down. Walls have ears, and officers have patrols."

The reality crashed back in, a physical, suffocating weight. The weight of the trench walls pressing in. The weight of the Colonel's order, still hanging over them like a suspended blade. The weight of the hopeless, stupid fantasy he'd just been clinging to like a drowning man to splinters. There was no escape. No barns. No silent, starry wilderness where war was a rumour. There was only this dugout, this trench, this unending, grinding present.

The shame was hot and immediate, burning Tommy's cheeks. The fantasy had been a moment of madness, a crack in his sanity he'd tumbled through. He had never left. He had sat here, on this platform he'd built, and dreamed the whole desperate journey while the cats slept and the sentries changed watch. The crushing totality of his powerlessness settled over him, heavier than any greatcoat, more constricting than the mud.

"Sorry," Tommy croaked, pushing himself up on an elbow. His body ached with a real, profound exhaustion that the dream-sleep had done nothing to alleviate.

His comrade just looked at him for a long moment, his expression a complex map of fatigue, understanding, and a flicker of the same desperate hope, quickly suppressed. Then he nodded, once, a sharp, economical movement. "Dawn's in an hour. Mackay's doing the rounds." The unspoken message was clear as day: *Get a grip. The dream's over. We're still here. All of us.*

The man melted back into the shadows of the crowded dugout. Tommy looked down at Penny. She stared back, her green eyes reflecting the dying candle flame like chips of bottle glass. She had been in the dream with him. But she was here, in the real, condemned world. She knew the difference. She had always known the difference between a safe cranny and a deadly open space. He was the one who had forgotten.

He had tried, in the last refuge of his mind, to desert. To save them. And he had failed without even moving a muscle. The trench had him. It had all of them. It allowed the fantasy only to make the waking truth more bitter.

Tommy watched the light seep into the dugout, a slow, grey stain that outlined the empty bully beef tins, the stacked rifles, the platform. He memorized it all: the way the straw was indented by four small bodies, the particular gnaw-mark on the corner of an ammo box crate made by The Major teething, the faint, lingering scent of condensed milk and cat.

The summons came just after stand-to, as the men were shuffling back from the firestep, rubbing life into cold hands. It came not with drama, but with the grim, bureaucratic certainty of Sergeant Mackay's arrival at their alcove. The Colonel's edict had not been forgotten, merely processed. Now, with the line static, the machinery of military tidiness ground into its final, remorseless phase.

Mackay's face was grey stone. "Today, Finch," he said, his voice low, stripped of all inflection. "RAVC detachment. They're to collect them. For disposal." He used the official word, the one from the paper, making it sound even colder.

The block of ice that had formed in Tommy's chest during the night solidified. This was not the shock of a new horror, but the chilling confirmation of the inevitable. The fantasy of the crater had been the last, feverish gasp of hope. This was the wake-up call, the alarm that couldn't be ignored.

He looked at Mackay, then past him to the platform. The fantasy was over. Only the reckoning remained.

"There's no appeal, Sarge?" The question was rote, a formality. "They've... they've saved our bacon more than once."

Mackay shook his head, a short, sharp, final

The Trench Cat of Ypres

movement. "It's logged. Hygiene. Discipline." The words were empty shells. They both knew the truth: it was about the offence of their existence to a man with clean boots.

Tommy nodded. A soldier accepting a death sentence for his platoon. "Understood, Sergeant."

Mackay hesitated. For a second, he was just an old, tired man in a mud-stiffened uniform. Then he placed a hand briefly, heavily, on Tommy's shoulder. The touch was electric, conveying a universe of shared powerlessness, of apology for a world that allowed this. Then the mask of the NCO slid back, and he was gone.

Tommy had the morning. One last morning.

He didn't try to smuggle them out. The dream had shown him the absurdity of that. The trench network was a sealed trap. He was a soldier. They were condemned. Their fates were locked together.

He spent the time in a strange, lucid trance. He performed the morning chores—checking his rifle, rolling his puttees—with robotic precision. But his mind was a recording device, capturing. The precise angle of Rust's ear when he heard a rat in the wall. The methodical, patting inspection Ginger gave to a new sandbag. The ridiculous, puff-chested strut of The Major after a successful bug-hunt. The exact weight and texture of Penny's head under his palm, the way she would press up into his touch.

That final hour, he shared his own breakfast with them —the fatty bits from the stew, a crust of bread soaked in the last of the condensed milk. He watched them play, the kittens tumbling in a pile of limbs and tails, Penny watching with that weary, fond gaze. He stroked her as she sat beside him, her body tense, reading the doom in the stillness of his hands, the silence where his usual, soft chatter should be.

He willed the cat and her kittens to run, to vanish into some corner of the line even he could not reach, so that he might look his seniors in the eye and truthfully say he did not know where they were. But there was nowhere left to go. Perhaps even the cats knew this, in their own uncanny way. It was the end.

When the kittens, worn out, finally slept in a purring heap, Tommy took out his pencil and the last clean scrap of paper from his paybook. He didn't write to his mother. What could he say that wouldn't break her or be censored into nonsense? Instead, he wrote to Mikey Doyle, the American ambulance driver with the easy laugh, who'd shared a cigarette with him in the rain after Passchendaele. He addressed it care of the American Ambulance Hospital, a message launched into the void.

The words came slowly, carved into the poor paper.

"Mikey, if you get this—

They're putting down the cats today. Penny, and her three kittens. My cats, though I never meant to have any. It just happened that way, same as everything else out here.

There's a grey tabby with more courage than sense. We call him The Major, on account of how he marches about like he owns the place. There's a clever ginger who watches everything, and a quiet one who sleeps unless there's work to be done. And their mother. Penny. She's the best of us all. Knows when to keep still. Knows when to move. Knows when not to be afraid. Knows when there's going to be a gas attack and saved my bacon more than once.

I won't pretend I don't understand why it's being done. Everything here has a reason, if you stand

> back far enough. But that doesn't make it easier to watch, or easier to carry.
>
> If you ever tell that story of the dog, Corporal—about how it stayed with you through the shelling and followed you half the length of France—maybe tell a small one about a cat too. Nothing grand. Just that in this place, for a while, there was a family. That they kept the rats down and the men company. That they belonged here as much as any of us did.
>
> Just so it's said. Just so it doesn't pass without a word.
>
> Thanks, mate.
>
> —Tommy"

He didn't know if it would ever be posted, or found, or read. It was a note in a bottle, tossed into a sea of mud. He folded it small and tucked it into a tin in his tunic pocket, over his heart.

The RAVC men arrived mid-morning. Two privates and a corporal, they looked uncomfortable and out of place, their uniforms less caked with the particular grime of the front line. They carried the tools of their trade: a heavy, dun-coloured canvas sack and a small, ominous wooden box with a metal clasp. They had the weary, dutiful air of men tasked with a necessary but distasteful bit of business.

"Sergeant says you have the animals here," the Corporal said, not unkindly, avoiding direct eye contact.

Tommy just pointed to the platform, his throat sealed shut.

The kittens, roused by the strangers, sensed the wrongness. The Major puffed up and hissed, a tiny, spitting statue of outrage. Rust vanished behind the crate.

Ginger stood stiff-legged beside her mother. Penny placed herself squarely between the men and her family, a low, continuous growl building in her throat—a sound Tommy had never heard from her before, raw and protective.

"Easy now, missus," one of the privates murmured, taking a hesitant step forward with the sack gaping open.

"Wait." Tommy's voice was flat, dead. He stepped forward. "I'll do it."

The corporal looked relieved, nodding quickly. "If you're sure. Quick and clean, that's the way. It's chloroform. They won't feel a thing." He said it like a mercy.

Tommy took the sack. It smelled of hemp and dust and the faint, sweet-chemical scent of what was to come. He approached the platform. Penny's growl stopped. She looked at him, and in her eyes was no accusation, no betrayal. There was only a deep, weary, exhausted understanding. She had seen men come and go. She had heard the orders given in that tone of voice. She knew what the sack meant.

"I'm sorry," he whispered, the words less than ash. He moved fast, because to hesitate was to shatter into a million unmendable pieces.

* * *

When it was done, the sack was closed.

Tommy handed it to the corporal. It was heavier than it should have been. The man took it, his face grim, hefting it slightly. The box with the chloroform and rags remained unopened. The corporal nodded to his men, and they turned to leave, the sack swinging between them like a dreadful pendulum, bumping against the corporal's leg.

Tommy didn't watch them go. He stared at the empty

platform. At the bit of frayed rope. At the perfect, small dents in the straw. The dugout was suddenly vast, hollow, and silent in a way it had never been. The constant, comforting background rustle and squeak and purr of life was gone, erased.

The silence was absolute.

It was the sound of the war, having finally noticed and extinguished a small, unauthorized spark..

He turned mechanically. He picked up his rifle, the wood cold and familiar. He climbed to the firestep, taking his place in the line of grey-faced men. He looked out at the wasted land, the wire, the mist. The war stretched on, infinitely, in all directions. It had won. It always won.

There was no great, heroic charge afterwards, no meaningful sacrifice. A week later, during a routine evening strafe—a desultory exchange of artillery that meant nothing—a random German whizz-bang shell landed squarely on the parapet of Tommy's section. It was the kind of blind, stupid, anonymous death that was the true currency of the trench. One moment he was there, a silent, hollow figure staring into the gloom. The next, there was a flash, a roar of earth, and then nothing.

When the dust settled, they pulled three bodies from the rubble. They were indistinguishable, caked in chalk and mud.

His few effects were gathered by a weary lieutenant: dog tags, paybook, and an unsent, crumpled letter to Mikey Doyle from the tin in his tunic pocket. The lieutenant smoothed the paper and read it by the flicker of a storm lantern. He shrugged—a small, helpless movement—then folded it again, now stained with mud and something darker.

He filed the letter and the tin away with a thousand other fragments of unfinished lives, intending to pass it on when there was time.

There never was.

A shell took his dugout days later, and everything went back into the mud.

But before then, somewhere, in the smoky warmth of a dugout, or around a brazier during a lull, the story was told. Not a grand story. A small, sad, whispered story. About a private from Durham. About a scruffy ginger cat he bought for a shilling. About a tiny pocket of life, made and held for a little while, in the very heart of the death-factory. About how it ended, not with a bang, but with a bureaucratic order and a canvas sack.

It was a story without glory, without a hero's death, without any meaning at all that could be carved on stone. Except the one every soldier who heard it, who had ever shared his last biscuit with a ratter or felt a pang for a dying horse, understood in his bones: that in the midst of the great, grinding, impersonal horror, the desperate, futile, beautiful act of caring for something—of preserving a tiny, unauthorized spark of life—was the last, fragile shred of what made you human. Before the vast, indifferent machinery of it all swallowed you whole.

It wasn't a victory.

It was just a truth. As small, and as sharp, and as enduring as a claw-mark on a sandbag, fading slowly under the endless, indifferent rain.

Epilogue: The Tin

The war ended, as all things must, not with a bang that shook the Salient, but with a silence that fell across it like a tired blanket. Men climbed out of trenches and walked home, or tried to. The guns were dragged away. The wire was collected for scrap. The great, festering wound of the front began, slowly, to scar over.

In a field near what had been the support lines, where the mud had once been churned by a million boots, a farmer named Arnaud bent to his work. His plough, turning the earth for the first time in years, struck something hard and metallic. He knelt, brushing away the cold, wet soil.

It was a British helmet, rusted through, its liner long gone to mulch. And beside it, partly fused to the rust by time and pressure, was a small, corroded tin—the kind that held tobacco or ointment. Arnaud pried it open with his thumbnail. Inside, protected from the worst of the damp by the tin's seal, was a scrap of paper, folded tight. The pencil marks were faded but still legible. His French was poor, his English worse, but he understood *cat*, and *three*, and the word *family*. He saw a name: *Tommy*. He saw the desperate, careful handwriting of a man trying to make something permanent.

Arnaud did not throw it back. The farmer, whose own barn cats kept the rats from his grain, read it slowly, his lips moving. He didn't understand all the words, but he understood the sentiment. He did not know the man, but he knew the land. He knew what it had swallowed. He would never know the colour of the cat's fur, or the sound of her purr. But for a moment, standing in the cold spring rain, he held the weight of the story in his hand

He placed the helmet and the tin carefully on the stone wall at the edge of his field, near the wild roses that grew where no trench had been. At the end of the day, he took the tin home, washed the mud from it, and placed it on the mantle beside a photograph of his own father, lost at the Marne.

Years passed. The field grew wheat, then barley. Arnaud grew old. The tin moved from the mantle to a drawer, and when he died, it passed to his daughter, Marie, who kept it for her father's sake, though she'd never known why he valued a rusty tin.

Decades later, Marie's grandson, Luc, was clearing her attic in Ypres. The tin was in a box of "old metal things." Luc, a history teacher, opened it. The paper was brittle now, the folds threatening to tear. He read it under the attic's bare bulb, translating slowly. The story emerged, line by fragile line: a cat named Penny, three kittens, a soldier who only wanted it said.

It was a tiny, heartbreaking artifact. Not of strategy or glory, but of the heart's lonely economy in the midst of industrial slaughter. Luc didn't put it on eBay with the other militaria. He took it to the local museum, the one in the Cloth Hall that documented the lives, not just the deaths, of the Salient.

The archivist, a woman with kind eyes, handled the paper with white cotton gloves. "It's rare," she said softly. "Most of what we have is official. Diaries, sometimes. But this... this is a plea. A small act of witness.

They displayed it not in a grand case, but in a quiet corner of the "Personal Effects" room, next to a carved

The Trench Cat of Ypres

wooden bird and a water-stained love letter. The tin was there, open, with the fragile paper inside. The caption read simply:

> *Found near Boesinghe, 1919. A note carried by a British soldier, concerning a cat and her kittens in the trenches. A request that they be remembered.*

Visitors passed by. Some paused. Some read it, their eyes softening. A child pointed and asked her mother what it said. The mother read it aloud, her voice dropping to a whisper by the end.

Others stood longer than they meant to, eyes bright, unsettled. It seemed that the small life of a cat, and her kitten, reached them in a way the countless human names sometimes did not—perhaps because it was simpler, or because it asked nothing in return.

Outside the museum, the rain fell on Ypres, as it always had. It fell on the rebuilt Cloth Hall, on the Menin Gate with its endless names, on the quiet fields where poppies still grew in the disturbed earth. And in a quiet corner, under glass, a soldier's last, fragile duty was finally done. The story had been kept. It had been said.

It wasn't a victory. It was a whisper, passed from the earth to a farmer, from a drawer to a teacher, from a scrap of paper to anyone who cared to listen.

A whisper about a pennyworth of luck, and the small, fierce things we try to save, even when we cannot save ourselves.

AUTHOR'S NOTE

Cats were a common presence in the trenches of the First World War, though their status was inconsistent and rarely formalised. Many were kept unofficially by soldiers as ratters, companions, or mascots; others were deliberately retained or introduced by military authorities for pest control in trenches, dugouts, depots, and ships. In practice, their presence was often sanctioned, tolerated, or quietly supported, even when it fell outside regulation.

They were valued primarily as ratters, but also as companions and morale anchors, and—according to many soldiers' accounts—as early warning systems, reacting to shellfire or gas before men could. Cats appear in photographs, letters, and memoirs, usually mentioned only in passing, as part of the background texture of trench life.

No comprehensive records were kept. Cats were not issued, systematically enlisted, or consistently counted. Unlike horses or war dogs, their presence was never formally documented, and no reliable figures exist for how many lived in the trench systems of the Western Front, or how many died there. Their lives passed largely without official notice.

This tolerance was not absolute. Animals existed at the discretion of command and circumstance. Cats were permitted when useful, removed when inconvenient, and in some cases destroyed on grounds of hygiene, discipline, or logistical control. The same system that allowed them to remain could also decide they must be eliminated.

The events described in this book are grounded in the documented conditions of the Ypres Salient in 1917: the mud, the vermin, the weather, the routines of trench life, and the arbitrary violence of artillery. The story that unfolds here is one of countless small, private experiences that left little or no trace in the historical record.

This book is offered in recognition of those overlooked presences, and of the fragile bonds that existed in places where survival was often a matter of chance.

Lest we forget all who were lost.

www.ingramcontent.com/pod-product-compliance
Lightning Source LLC
Chambersburg PA
CBHW030331080526
44584CB00012B/808